CW01512255

"I wish this book had existed years ago. I
as a scholarly author; and it's the book ‚ₒ... .ₑₑₐ ₜₒₒ. rortwood-Stacer provides a
clearly drawn series of steps you can take to improve your own book (or article)
manuscript—to hone its arguments, its structure, and its style. If you want your
manuscript to be the best it can possibly be, *Make Your Manuscript Work* is the book
for you."

—STEPHEN B. HEARD, author of *The Scientist's Guide to Writing*

"In this gracefully written book, Laura Portwood-Stacer supplies meticulous, action-
able recommendations for the developmental editing of scholarly books, articles,
and theses, along with an array of useful exercises, examples, templates, and references. The author's 'four pillars of scholarly writing'—argument, evidence, structure, and style—provide an indispensable framework for all academic writers."

—HELEN SWORD, author of *Writing with Pleasure*

"Most writers, including many scholars, struggle with assessing and revising their
own work. While they know a text needs work, they don't typically have a systematic approach to making the necessary improvements. *Make Your Manuscript
Work* is designed to address this need, offering a detailed, practical, and clear overview of the process of scholarly editing that is grounded in Portwood-Stacer's extensive professional experience. Drawing on her respectful and sensitive approach
to both texts and relationships, Portwood-Stacer has written an essential guide to
scholarly editing."

—RACHAEL CAYLEY, author of *Thriving as a Graduate Writer*

MAKE YOUR MANUSCRIPT WORK

SKILLS FOR SCHOLARS

For a full list of titles in the series, go to https://press.princeton
.edu/series/skills-for-scholars.

Make Your Manuscript Work: A Guide to Developmental Editing for Scholarly Writers, Laura Portwood-Stacer

How to Mentor Anyone in Academia, Maria LaMonaca Wisdom

On the Art and Craft of Doing Science, Kenneth Catania

Academic Writing as if Readers Matter, Leonard Cassuto

Thinking through Writing: A Guide to Becoming a Better Writer and Thinker, John Kaag and Jonathan van Belle

The Pocket Instructor: Writing: 50 Exercises for the College Classroom, Edited by Amanda Irwin Wilkins and Keith Shaw

Stellar English: A Down-to-Earth Guide to Grammar and Style, Frank L. Cioffi

Try to Love the Questions: From Debate to Dialogue in Classrooms and Life, Lara Hope Schwartz

The Elements of Visual Grammar: A Designer's Guide for Writers, Scholars, and Professionals, Angela Riechers

Writing with Pleasure, Helen Sword

The Grant Writing Guide: A Road Map for Scholars, Betty S. Lai

The Secret Syllabus: A Guide to the Unwritten Rules of College Success, Jay Phelan and Terry Burnham

Writing on the Job: Best Practices for Communicating in the Digital Age, Martha B. Coven

The Economist's Craft: An Introduction to Research, Publishing, and Professional Development, Michael S. Weisbach

The Book Proposal Book: A Guide for Scholarly Authors, Laura Portwood-Stacer

Make Your Manuscript Work

A GUIDE TO DEVELOPMENTAL
EDITING FOR
SCHOLARLY WRITERS

LAURA PORTWOOD-STACER

PRINCETON UNIVERSITY PRESS

PRINCETON *&* OXFORD

Princeton University Press is committed to the protection of copyright
and the intellectual property our authors entrust to us. Copyright
promotes the progress and integrity of knowledge created by humans.
By engaging with an authorized copy of this work, you are supporting
creators and the global exchange of ideas. As this work is protected by
copyright, any reproduction or distribution of it in any form for any
purpose requires permission; permission requests should be sent to
permissions@press.princeton.edu. Ingestion of any PUP IP for any
AI purposes is strictly prohibited.

Published by Princeton University Press
41 William Street, Princeton, New Jersey 08540
99 Banbury Road, Oxford OX2 6JX

press.princeton.edu

GPSR Authorized Representative: Easy Access System Europe - Mustamäe
tee 50, 10621 Tallinn, Estonia, gpsr.requests@easproject.com

All Rights Reserved

Library of Congress Control Number: 2025934786
ISBN 9780691257471
ISBN (pbk.) 9780691257464
ISBN (e-book) 9780691257488

British Library Cataloging-in-Publication Data is available

Editorial: Matt Rohal, Alena Chekanov
Production Editorial: Elizabeth Byrd
Jacket: Karl Spurzem
Production: Erin Suydam
Publicity: Tyler Hubbert (US), Kathryn Stevens (UK)
Copyeditor: Rebecca Faith

Jacket/Cover Credit: Tavarius / Shutterstock

Printed in the United States of America

10 9 8 7 6 5 4 3 2 1

To Windsor and Walker

CONTENTS

Introduction: How to Develop a Scholarly
Manuscript   1

What Is Manuscript Development?   3

*Who Can Use the Method? On What Kinds of
Texts? When?*   9

How I Think About Manuscripts and Publishing   12

PHASE I. CLARIFY YOUR MISSION   17

1   Three Moments for Manuscript Development   19

*Moment 1: Development Before Submission To
Publishers*   23

Moment 2: Development After Peer Review   25

*Moment 3: Development After Approval for
Publication*   27

*Use an Author Questionnaire to Clarify Your
Mission in Manuscript Development*   30

2   Delineate Your Goals, Timeline, and Capacity   34

Clarifying Your Goals   35

Clarifying Your Timeline   38

Clarifying Your Capacity 41

*Use an Author Questionnaire to Clarify Your
Mission in Manuscript Development, Part 2* 43

PHASE II. ASSESS YOUR TEXT 47

3 Read Your Manuscript Like an Editor 49

Marking Up the Text 49

*Taking Your Time or Truncating the Assessment
Process* 51

Opportunities Versus Problems 54

4 Opportunities to Develop Your Argument 56

Give Your Text an Argument 58

*Distinguish Your Main Argument from Subordinate
Arguments and Other Types of Claims* 60

Make Your Argument Portable 63

*Sharpen Your Argument by Defining Your Main
Concepts* 65

*Solidify Your Contribution by Aligning the Scope of
Your Argument with the Interests of Your Intended
Readers* 66

5 Opportunities to Develop Your Evidence 69

Support All Arguments with Evidence 70

*Provide Only As Much Support As Your Arguments
Need* 72

*Present Sufficient and Reasonable Analysis of All
Evidence* 75

6 Opportunities to Develop Your Structure   78

   Create a Strong Sense of Narrative with Your Book's
   Table of Contents   79

   Organize Your Material in a Logical Flow at the
   Section and Paragraph Level   82

   Consider Conventions When Deciding How to
   Organize Your Book into Parts   85

   Use Titles, Headings, and Topic Sentences to Signal
   Content and Purpose to the Reader   87

   Use Breaks and Transitions to Signal Relationships
   Between Parts of the Text   91

   Shorten or Lengthen Your Text to Align with
   Reader Needs and Publisher Requirements   93

7 Opportunities to Develop Your Style   97

   Foreground Your Own Ideas   99

   Make Considered Choices About Notes   101

   Strike a Consistent and Appropriate Tone   102

   Clear Up Sentence-Level Obfuscations   106

   A Few Words of Encouragement   111

PHASE III. PLAN AND EXECUTE YOUR EDITS   115

8 Draft Your Editorial Summary   119

   The Content of Your Editorial Summary   121

   Close Your Summary by Listing Next Steps in
   Order of Priority   127

9　Itemize Your Edits　　131

　　How to Itemize Your Edits　　132

　　Keeping Edits in Scope with Your Plan　　137

10　Alter Your Text　　141

　　Five Tips for Executing Your Edits　　141

　　After the Developmental Edit　　143

　　Your Role in the Production Process　　146

Conclusion: Let Your Manuscript Do Its Work　　151

Acknowledgments　155

*Appendix A. Checklist of Opportunities and
Assessment Questions*　159

Appendix B. Sample Editorial Materials　165

*Appendix C. Supportive Readers in
Manuscript Development*　195

*Appendix D. Using This Book's Method to
Support Other Writers*　209

Notes　227

Bibliography　235

Index　239

MAKE YOUR MANUSCRIPT WORK

How to Develop a Scholarly Manuscript

"IT FEELS like a handful of people, somewhere, must understand how academic publishing works," said a participant in a workshop I recently held for academic writers. "The rest of us are just trying to figure it out as we go and hoping we get it right." As a professional developmental editor for scholarly authors, I've heard similar sentiments expressed countless times. The scholar in this instance is a tenured professor at a research university who has published multiple well-received books and half a dozen peer-reviewed articles. From the outside, she looks like a successful academic writer, yet she still lacks certainty about the steps that lead to such success.

The problem with uncertainty is that it breeds anxiety, which prevents many scholars from moving forward with their writing projects as quickly as they want to. If you're unsure what publishers are looking for, you'll dither over whether your manuscript is ready to submit. If you don't know what to expect from the revision process, you may be stymied by perfectionism before you even finish a full draft. Some scholars eventually learn how to write and publish through trial and error, but doing so takes time, social capital, and emotional fortitude, all of which are in short supply these days.

Even after you've resolved to send your manuscript to a publisher, the uncertainty continues. What if peer reviewers don't understand the point of your project? What if you receive conflicting feedback? Will you have to spend years revising in order to get published? As you get pulled through the process, you can feel as if you're no longer the one in charge of your own ideas, but instead you're just trying to get other people to deem your work good enough to be shared with the world. It's no wonder the writing and publishing process can feel so stressful and disempowering for scholarly authors.

This book is here to help academic writers reclaim a bit of agency. You won't be able to control everything, because you can't know in advance whether a specific publisher will want to invest in your manuscript or whether peer reviewers will support what you're trying to do. You can't force readers to cite your ideas or compel committees to give you recognition and awards. But you can learn how to present your research in ways that meet the needs of scholarly publishers and readers, increasing your chances of having your text resonate with those you most want to reach. And you can come to understand how manuscripts travel through the publishing process and use that knowledge to make your own decisions about what your text will be.

I aim to empower you by offering a systematic method you can use to develop your manuscripts in progress, taking them from first drafts to well-formed, publishable texts. This method is derived from my decade of experience working as a developmental editor for academic authors. After helping hundreds of writers refine their book projects and land contracts with their dream publishers, I want to help more scholars reap the benefits of developmental editing for themselves. If that sounds intriguing to you, you're in the right place.

What Is Manuscript Development?

Perhaps you only recently became aware that developmental editors exist, maybe even as recently as when you read the previous paragraph. The question is: What do they do? Developmental editors work on texts at a crucial stage: after the text has been conceptualized and drafted, but before it gets polished at the level of sentences, words, and punctuation. Developmental editing deals with the most fundamental aspects of a text. Different editors will describe these aspects with different terms, but for me, these aspects can be typologized as argument, evidence, structure, and style, which I call the **four pillars of scholarly writing** (Figure 1.1).

How do developmental editors approach these four pillars? First, we clarify the **argument** that's driving the text, the author's core claim that will cause a change to the reader's understanding of the subject matter. In scholarly writing, a writer's argument is often their text's novel contribution to a field and is the text's main reason to exist, so it must be clear. Next, we developmental editors ensure that the writer has backed up their argument appropriately with well-analyzed **evidence** and that they are using the **structure** of their text to guide the reader's understanding of the argument. Finally, we consider the text's **style**, looking at how the writer's overall attitude to both subject and reader shows up on the page. Developmental editors don't check for correct grammar or even elegant prose, as a line editor would. The aim is rather to help the writer project a consistent voice that earns credibility with their intended audience.

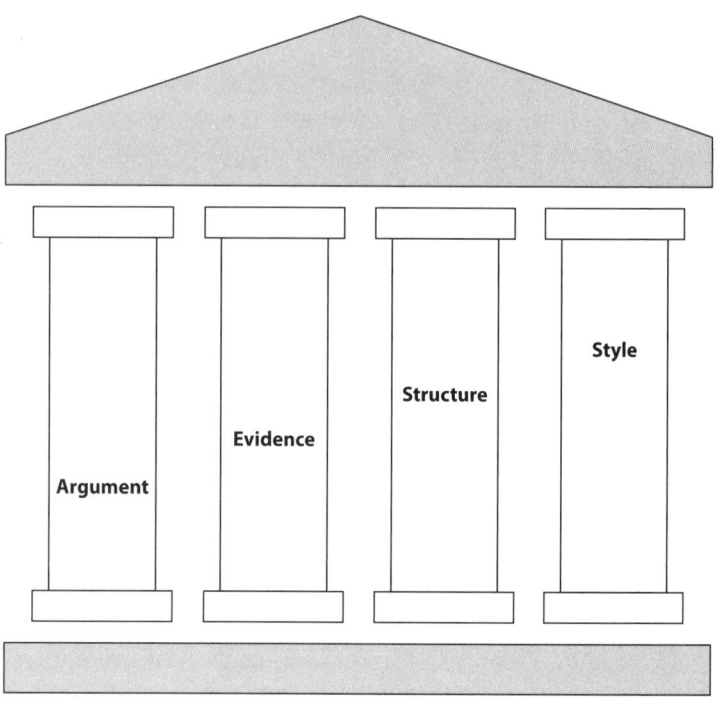

FIGURE I.1. The four pillars of scholarly writing

Scholarly manuscripts must have a solid foundation in all four areas to be successful in the publishing process. Each of these fundamental aspects of the text has the potential to make or break the text's chances of being received well by peer reviewers, getting approved for publication, and ultimately reaching readers in the author's scholarly field and beyond. Although elegant prose and correct grammar are worthy aspirations, publication decisions and reader reception of academic texts tend to hinge less on technical perfection than on the big-picture aspects of argument, evidence, structure, and overall style. Developing your manuscript's fundamentals is therefore imperative, both before you submit it for consideration by publishers, and before your text goes out into the world upon publication. You've likely paid attention to argument, evidence, structure, and style in your writing, though you may not have used the same exact terms or described your big-picture revisions as developmental editing. Yet if you're like most writers I've met, you've lacked an organized system for evaluating these fundamentals in your own manuscripts in progress. I've noticed that most academic writing advice focuses either on establishing a regular writing practice to get drafts done or on tightening up prose at the level of paragraphs and sentences. Writers are rarely taught a methodical approach to the crucial stage between drafting and polishing. Few scholars know that developmental editing is a thing, fewer know what it involves, and even fewer know how to do it for their own manuscripts in a systematic way.

As a remedy for this situation, this book offers a novel framework that academic writers can apply to their own manuscripts in progress: the **manuscript development cycle**. The manuscript development cycle consists of three phases that mirror the work I do with scholarly authors as a professional developmental editor (Figure 1.2).

Phase I involves **clarifying your mission** in developing the manuscript. You'll establish the basic parameters of the text you want to publish in terms of topic, scope, and research approach. You'll also identify your intended readers and the publisher you hope to partner with. Clarity on your mission further entails taking stock of where your manuscript currently stands with potential publishers. Are you preparing the manuscript for initial submission, hoping to make it to the peer review stage? Do you already have feedback from acquiring editors and peer reviewers that you'll be using to develop the text further? In Phase I, you'll also define the work you want your manuscript to do in the world

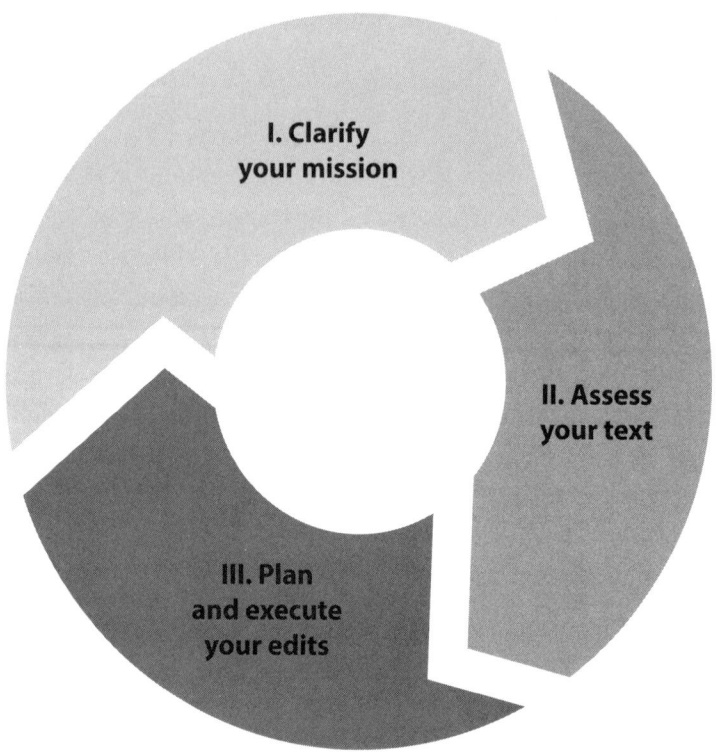

FIGURE I.2. The manuscript development cycle

after publication. Is the text supposed to anchor your tenure file, garner public recognition for your research, or support a community that can benefit from your knowledge? Finally, getting a full picture of your mission in developing your manuscript involves an inventory of the resources available to you. How much time and capacity do you have to develop the text further? Clarifying your mission in undertaking manuscript development isn't difficult, but many authors take their mission for granted or don't realize they should pause to make key decisions about their text before they invest more time in working on it.

Phase II of the manuscript development cycle involves **assessing your text** in its current form to identify opportunities to strengthen its four pillars. Assessment means reading the text critically, evaluating how its argument, evidence, structure, and style are presented across the entire draft. In this phase of the cycle you will diagnose your text's weaknesses and recognize its strengths.

Phase III involves **planning and executing edits** to your text. In this phase, you'll filter your initial reactions from the assessment phase and organize your thoughts into an editorial summary. Crafting an editorial summary requires you to decide which aspects of the text need to be developed further to achieve the aims articulated in Phase I. It also means itemizing and prioritizing specific edits you'll make in light of the time and resources you have available. Once you have a concrete plan in place that allows you to take control over what changes you will make and when, you'll execute your edits, arriving at a draft that's ready to move along to the next stage of the publishing process.

Most authors skip directly to executing edits when setting out to revise a draft, missing the vital work of clarifying, assessing, and planning. By systematically rotating through the whole manuscript development cycle, you'll avoid the directionless tinkering that keeps so many writers stuck. You'll not only know what to do, but you'll also have a much better sense of why to do it and when. Completing the manuscript development cycle takes time—time to learn it by reading this book and time to apply it to your manuscript in progress. But this investment of time will pay off exponentially as you become a more powerful editor of your work and move through the publishing process with greater confidence and efficiency.

The manuscript development cycle is a tool that will enable you to edit your own work before you ever send it out for feedback. It will also empower you to make your own decisions about your text once you have external feedback in hand, even when that feedback is incomplete or contradictory. Furthermore, the cycle will give you insights into your writing that will help you with future manuscripts. Having this tool at your disposal will make new writing projects feel less daunting because you'll know that you have a reliable method for making them publishable once you have a rough draft down.

I call it the manuscript development **cycle** because a writer may rotate through the phases several times between first draft and final version. As I will discuss in Chapter 1, an author is called upon to make substantive improvements to their manuscript at a few **key moments in the typical publishing timeline**:

- **Moment 1**: preparing for initial submission to publishers
- **Moment 2**: revising after receiving feedback from preliminary readers but before receiving publication approval, for example, responding to peer reviews in hope of acceptance
- **Moment 3**: preparing the final manuscript to go into production

You'll benefit from passing through all three phases of manuscript development at each of these moments. The cycle is also scalable to specific parts of a text; for instance, after completing the cycle for an entire book manuscript, you may want to repeat the cycle for a particular chapter that needs extra attention before moving your manuscript to the next publishing stage.

I've chosen the term *development* for particular reasons too. Some might point out that what I've already described could be called revision, rewriting, or simply writing. However, revision is often used to refer to finer levels of prose polishing in which a writer makes minute decisions about sentence structure, word choice, and other aesthetic features of a text. Although some definitions of revision include the kind of fundamental development I'm talking about here, I think having a more specific term for this particular stage of the writing and revision process can help authors gain more clarity about what they need to do for their manuscript at any given time. Polishing your prose will have its hour, but separating that work from your developmental work can save effort and put your attention where it's needed, when it's needed. By calling this work *developmental*, I'm also building on the existing terminology that the publishing industry already uses to distinguish between the levels of editing that occur at various points in the publishing process, with developmental editing always preceding line editing, copyediting, and proofreading.[1]

The term *development* further appeals to me because it entails an implicit acknowledgment that every text will necessarily grow and change between its moment of conception and its final publication. No publishable text initially lands on the page in its complete form, and all ideas must be nurtured and cultivated with intention before they're ready to go out into the world and do the work we want them to do. Having a manuscript in need of development doesn't mean you're a bad writer. It simply means you're a writer.

Who Can Use the Method? On What Kinds of Texts? When?

The framework of manuscript development can be used by scholarly writers at every career stage, in every field, and for every type of manuscript. However, in the interest of concreteness, I'm going to show you how to apply the method to scholarly book manuscripts specifically. I'll be speaking directly from my experience helping academic writers publish research-based books in the humanities and qualitative social sciences with university presses and other publishers that serve the English-speaking academic market, mainly in the United States. Some of the advice and examples I offer will be specific to that context. The general contours of the manuscript development method, however, will be portable to other forms of academic writing, such as journal articles, theses, dissertations, seminar papers, conference presentations, fellowship applications, and grant proposals. I recommend using this book in conjunction with other guides to help you decode the specific expectations in your field and for the type of manuscript you're working on.[2]

All scholarly writers can find value in this book, but I had a few specific kinds of people in mind when I decided to write it. This book is particularly for writers who have high standards for their work but feel they lack the necessary tools to meet those standards. It's for scholars who have received less than comprehensive feedback on their writing from mentors who were too busy to help them learn the ropes of academic publishing. It's for aspiring authors who have had their work rejected by publishers while getting little guidance on what could be done to improve it. It's for first-generation academics, scholars from historically marginalized and underrepresented groups and regions, speakers of English as an additional language, and those in positions of precarious employment or unemployment. It's also for any writer who simply appreciates a step-by-step method for getting things done.

The method of self-editing in this book will be especially beneficial for people who, for valid reasons, have a hard time seeking outside help. You may worry that asking for assistance or sharing drafts at an early stage of development could confirm a misperception that you're incompetent or undeserving of your position, especially if you belong to a marginalized group. You may also fear plagiarism or others taking credit for your original ideas. You may have had negative experiences with feedback in the past that have left you hesitant to invite criticism of your work.[3] Professional developmental editing services can be a boon for such writers, but the cost of a professional's labor and expertise may be prohibitively expensive for many. Although no book can make up for those structural obstacles, I aim to give you tools to develop your work and take it as far as you can on your own. (If you do decide to seek outside support for developing your manuscripts in progress, Appendix C offers practical guidance on how to get that support.)

Last, this book is for people who support scholarly writers, though I'll mostly address such readers indirectly. The skills I share can be used by any editor, mentor, or colleague who provides feedback on another writer's text, such as

- Professors who mentor graduate students, advanced undergraduate writers, and early career faculty;
- Scholars who organize special journal issues or edited volumes;
- Book series editors and journal editors;
- Acquiring editors at scholarly publishers;
- Peer reviewers; and
- Freelance editors and literary agents who work with scholarly authors.

The aforementioned types of readers will be able to determine which advice is relevant to your role and can adapt everything else as needed. (For more specific guidance, Appendix D is addressed directly to readers who would like to use this book's method when giving feedback on other people's writing.)

The method I present is designed to be worked through step by step, but I welcome all readers to skim the entire book fully so you can get an overview of the work ahead of you before applying the method to your manuscript in progress. I also recommend waiting to implement the method until you have a full draft of your manuscript in hand, though it's okay if the draft has a few holes that you know will need filling. Can you clearly articulate your text's topic, scope, methodological and theoretical approaches, as well as your reason for writing the manuscript in the first place? If so, you're likely ready for manuscript development. If you're turning your dissertation into a book, you can count your dissertation as a draft and apply the method to it, with the awareness that quite a lot of development may be needed. As you become more practiced in the method of manuscript development, the principles will likely help you as you conceive and write new projects from scratch, but that application is beyond the scope of this book.[4]

How I Think About Manuscripts and Publishing

If you're still reading, I'm assuming you're intrigued by what this book offers. However, before ending this introduction, I want to briefly explain where I'm coming from and how I think about scholarly writing and publishing. Having read many other academic writing guides, I know how essential it is for readers to feel a sense of compatibility with an advice giver's outlook and voice.

I take a pragmatic approach to writing, editing, and publishing. I don't write or publish books for the inherent love of it, nor do I romanticize the creative output of the authors I work with. Many writers find deep meaning, personal fulfillment, and even pleasure in the writing process. Some take pride in producing well-crafted prose for its own sake. I admire those writers, but I'm not one of them. I don't expect all readers of this book to be those kinds of writers either.[5]

Scholarly manuscripts are the products of labor that can be leveraged for concrete goals. When I look at any given scholarly manuscript, I think about the work the author wants it to do in the world. This work can include communicating vital ideas to an audience of readers whose own lives and scholarship can benefit from the writer's intellectual contributions. A published book can also function as a token in the academic economy, where the fact that the book was published at all—or the fact that it was published by a particular press—can be as significant as its contents. A book is also a commodity, a product packaged and marketed to generate revenue for both publisher and author. A book can be a reputational calling card that leads to other opportunities such as media appearances, speaking gigs, and expert consulting work. You can probably think of other things you want your text to do. I don't judge any of these forms of work or consider any of them better or worse reasons to publish a scholarly manuscript. My approach is to meet you—the author—where you are, help you name your aspirations, and recognize that different amounts and types of labor will be needed from you to enable your manuscript to accomplish the work you want it to do.

In revealing the conventions and expectations of publishing gatekeepers and showing you how to meet them, my approach could be seen as fundamentally conservative. I don't attempt to radically question or transform institutions of scholarly publishing here. However, you have your own power and agency in the writing and publishing process. I hope to help you write the text you want to write, how you want to write it. You may need to develop your work in particular ways if you want certain publishers and readers to come along with you, but that will be up to you. If you're on a mission to reimagine what scholarly writing and publishing can be, I hope this book will help you do that too.

I'll speak to you openly as an experienced and supportive colleague. I've personally guided hundreds of aspiring authors through the process of writing scholarly books and book proposals, and thousands more scholars have benefited from my online programs, public seminars, and institutional workshops. My clients have published with every large university press in the United States, as well as with smaller publishers, commercial publishers, and international publishers.[6] I've also authored several journal articles and three academic books of my own, including a monograph based on my doctoral dissertation. Before setting up my editorial business in 2015, I earned a PhD in communication, held a five-year post as an associate editor at a scholarly journal in my field, and served as a peer reviewer for several journals and book publishers. Many of the lessons I share in this book were hard-won, learned from years of practice and missteps along the way.

I strive to provide a comprehensive picture of scholarly developmental editing practices and how they can be used by writers and those who support them, but I make no claims as to the universality of my methods among other developmental editors. My perspective is unavoidably shaped by my own subject positions, which include being American, a monolingual speaker of English, and a trainee in particular traditions of academic writing and knowledge production.

I make this offering not as the definitive expert on academic writing and publishing, but as someone with experience-informed knowledge I want others to benefit from. When I'm aware of other expert advice that I think may help you deal with a particular issue, I'll reference it in the endnotes. The notes thus collectively serve as a recommended reading list. I'll refrain from using notes for any other purpose, aside from citing the source of a quoted phrase from time to time. If you see a note indicated in the text, know that it doesn't point to a discursive digression. Consult the endnotes only if you're looking for additional resources and bibliographic information for the topic under discussion.

The method presented in this book isn't a rigid program. Even where I seem to offer prescriptive advice, I'm only doing so to give you a starting point and reduce your decision fatigue. The ways you apply—or choose not to apply—the guidance I offer will be unique, both because you bring your own set of perspectives to the table and because every manuscript presents its own opportunities for development. Use this book as a resource but be prepared for flexibility as you find what works for you and the other writers you support. I wish you the best of luck.

PHASE I

Clarify Your Mission

LATER PARTS of this book will help you diagnose and improve your manuscript based on its precise contents, but the starting point is to clarify your mission in writing and publishing your text. Gaining clarity on your mission will ensure that the developmental work you do is directed toward achieving your intended result. The needs and interests of publishers, readers, and yourself as the writer should all be considered to make your manuscript work the way you want it to.

Chapter 1 deals with the importance of readership as context for any developmental work you do on your manuscript. I'll lay out the typical journey that scholarly book manuscripts take through the publishing pipeline, noting what kind of development is called for at each stage, based on how, when, and by whom manuscripts are evaluated. In Chapter 2 I'll discuss how your own context as the writer may affect how much development you want to undertake and when. At the end of each chapter, a short questionnaire is included to help you clarify your intentions for your manuscript, setting you up to be a more effective editor of your own work.

Before you jump into the next two chapters, take a few minutes to reacquaint yourself with the manuscript you're currently working on. Scan your text to remind yourself of its topic, scope, approach, and purpose. But don't do a careful reread right now. Don't start trying to diagnose problems with how your ideas are presented. Definitely don't start editing your document! The time for all that will come later, after you learn the systematic method described in this book.

Once you've done your quick scan, come back and proceed to Chapter 1.

1

Three Moments for
Manuscript Development

THE WAY you write and develop any manuscript intended for publication will be informed by your need to reach two distinct sets of readers: **preliminary readers** and **end readers**. Preliminary readers are those who will encounter the text before it's finalized and accepted for publication. At scholarly book publishers, preliminary readers may include acquiring editors, series editors, peer reviewers, an internal editorial committee, a faculty editorial board, and other personnel such as marketers, publicists, and sales staff. These preliminary readers will provide input for, or directly participate in, decisions about whether the text will be published at all.[1] (Your prepublication readers can also include "friendly reviewers," beta readers, and even freelance editors who can help you develop your manuscript. These readers don't participate in decisions about publication, and I discuss them specifically in Appendix C.)

By end readers, I mean the people your text is ultimately written to reach and educate. This audience may encompass one or more of the following groups:

- expert scholars and graduate student researchers in your field or subfield
- scholars in adjacent fields or subfields
- undergraduate or graduate students completing coursework
- readers outside the academy in professional settings, activist circles, or other communities that matter to you
- nonacademic readers who have a personal interest in learning about your area of study

While your manuscript needs to win the support of preliminary readers to be published at all, it also needs to resonate with at least one well-defined set of end readers if it's to have any impact beyond the fact of its being published.

If my formulation of end readers feels a bit corporate to you, akin to the imagined end users of a new product undergoing research and development, that isn't accidental. Most academics read scholarship instrumentally, even if we authors might like to imagine readers taking intrinsic pleasure from spending time with our prose and ideas. Writing expert Leonard Cassuto likens academic readers to blue whales, observing that "When researchers read, they take in large amounts of information and strain out what they intend to use in their own work. Like blue whales, academic readers retain only what will benefit them."[2] This academic tendency to read for use value is why I encourage you to think about the "ends" to which you want your text to be put and shape your manuscript accordingly.

The needs and expectations of preliminary readers differ from the needs and expectations of end readers. Therefore, each moment during the publishing process calls on you to develop your manuscript with particular sets of readers in mind. At **Moment 1**, when preparing for initial submission to publishers, your most consequential readers will be acquiring editors and peer reviewers. At **Moment 2**, when revising after getting feedback from preliminary readers but before receiving publication approval, your editor and peer reviewers remain important readers, joined by your publisher's editorial board. At **Moment 3**, when preparing the final manuscript to go into production, you'll be developing your text with end readers at the forefront of your mind.

You'll repeat all three phases of the manuscript development cycle—clarifying your mission, assessing your text, and planning and executing edits—at each of these three moments, though you may do different amounts of work on your manuscript in each rotation through the cycle. If you receive positive feedback and few requested changes from peer reviewers, for example, you may have much less to do in terms of manuscript development at Moments 2 and 3 than you had at Moment 1. On the other hand, if you didn't develop your manuscript thoroughly at Moment 1, you may have a lot more to do at Moment 2 after getting feedback from peer reviewers. If you're fairly confident that your pre-submission manuscript is in good enough shape to satisfy peer reviewers, you may even strategically decide to do less development in the early stages so that you can do your deepest work on the manuscript at Moment 3, when preparing the text for your end readers (Figure 1.1).

I'll now discuss each moment in more detail so you can understand both how book manuscripts are evaluated at each stage of the publishing process and what to keep in mind as you undertake your manuscript development.[3]

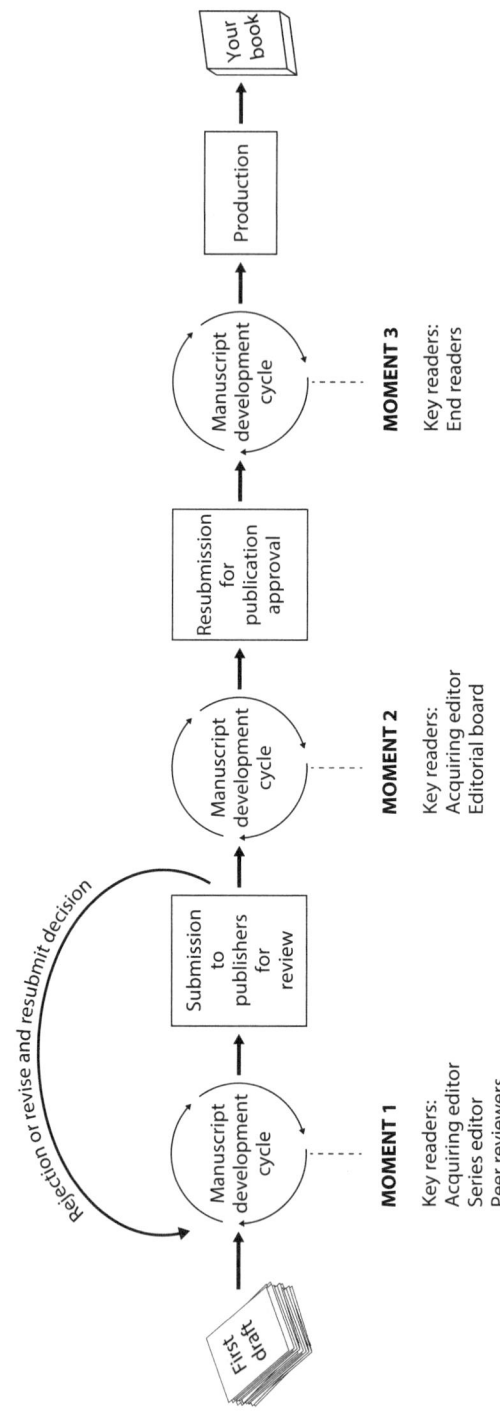

FIGURE 1.1. Three moments for manuscript development in the scholarly book publication process

Moment 1: Development Before Submission to Publishers

Your first preliminary reader at the press you want to publish with will be an acquiring editor or series editor. Acquiring editors are employed by publishers, and they bring books into the press, guiding both manuscript and author through all the stages of the publishing process. Acquiring editors often specialize in certain subject areas and are attuned to current conversations taking place in scholarly disciplines. Series editors are scholars who partner with publishers to acquire collections of books united by common themes. Series editors are often regarded as leading experts and are well-networked in their fields, allowing them to attract and evaluate book projects that will fit well in their series. Some books are published outside of series, and some series editors aren't active in recruitment, so you may or may not be dealing with a series editor in addition to an acquiring editor when approaching a publisher about your project.[4]

The first thing acquiring editors and series editors look for when evaluating a new project is a strong sense of fit with the scope of the series and the publisher's overall mission. Scholarly publishers develop strengths and reputations in specific areas, meaning that certain topics and research approaches resonate better at some presses than others. Specialization helps scholarly publishers reach promising target markets more efficiently, which is particularly urgent at small not-for-profit presses, such as university presses, where the staff is doing their best to market their books with limited resources. When initially considering your submission, preliminary readers at your publisher will thus be looking at whether your manuscript is aligned with their previous offerings or possibly with new areas of interest.

At this stage, presses will be considering your topic, the kinds of evidence and analysis you use to support your argument, and the length and basic structure of your manuscript.[5]

If your book is a plausible fit for the publisher or series, the acquiring editor or series editor will look for your book's original contribution to scholarly conversations currently happening in your field. Therefore, your book must present a compelling argument that will stimulate readers' thinking about both your specific topic and the broader concerns in your discipline and possibly beyond. Your editor may not have the scholarly expertise to evaluate everything. They'll depend on expert peer reviewers to assess the validity of your argument, whether it's adequately supported by evidence and analysis, and whether it makes a relevant contribution to your field. But your editor will want to see that you've articulated a clear argument in the first place before they'll be willing to enlist peer reviewers to comment on its soundness.

Before investing time and effort in securing peer reviewers, the acquiring editor also needs to believe that your book can appeal to a well-defined book-buying market. Therefore, in addition to looking for a significant scholarly contribution and a sense of fit with previously published books, acquiring editors will be looking at your overall writing style. Specifically, they'll assess whether your text's style is likely to appeal to a large enough readership to justify the press's financial investment in producing your book. Because university library budgets have been slashed, publishers can no longer count on standing orders for every research monograph they publish.[6] Many publishers are therefore working hard to get their books directly into the hands of readers via retail and other channels. Accordingly, publishers seek books that hold strong appeal for readers and for the booksellers and librarians who make individual purchase and stocking decisions. This focus on reader appeal means that scholarly books, more than ever, must be engagingly written and structured to reward the reader's time.

Once you clear the hurdle of getting an acquiring editor to see potential in your project, your manuscript will be sent to peer reviewers for further evaluation. Although it's impossible to predict how peer reviewers will react to your text, you'll greatly increase your chances of making a good impression if you do earnest developmental work on the manuscript's argument, evidence, structure, and style before it goes out to reviewers. However, don't aspire to absolute perfection before submitting your manuscript for review. Peer review is an important part of the manuscript development process, so everyone involved—publisher, reviewers, and author—should be open to the idea that the manuscript can and will evolve after this moment.[7]

Moment 2: Development After Peer Review

After your text is peer reviewed, you'll be presented with another opportunity to further develop your manuscript. How you approach this next rotation through the manuscript development cycle will depend heavily on the outcome of the first round of peer review. If things don't work out with the first publisher due to peer reviewers objecting to major aspects of your book's argument, evidence, structure, or style, you may want to develop your manuscript further before trying with another publisher. However, it could be that the first publisher simply wasn't a good fit for your project and thus didn't get suitable reviewers. If this is the case, you may want to be more careful about your selection process when choosing your next press and pause further manuscript development until you have a new set of peer reviews in hand.

Another possible outcome from the first round of peer review is that your editor may ask you to revise your text using the peer reviewer feedback and resubmit the manuscript for a second round of review before the editor will seek approval to offer you a publishing agreement. This outcome could happen if the peer reviewers see potential in your project but have major concerns they want to see addressed before they can fully endorse publication. Your manuscript may also be subject to further review if the first round of peer review was based on only a book proposal and sample chapters. Although some presses will issue an advance contract if the first round of peer reviews on the partial manuscript is positive, indicating the press's strong interest in publishing the book, most advance contracts stipulate that the full text must make it through another complete round of peer review before a final decision on publication can be made.[8] Whether you receive a revise-and-resubmit decision or an advance contract, you'll want to put your fully drafted text through the manuscript development cycle in preparation for the next round of peer review. You'll have an advantage as you go through the cycle this time, because you'll know which aspects of your manuscript need the most attention based on feedback from the first round of peer review.

Although peer review can play an important role in manuscript development, peer reviewers aren't developmental editors nor are they expected to be. You may have to read between the lines of their comments and use your peer review reports in conjunction with this book to figure out how to address some of the concerns reviewers raise. Because most manuscripts are read by at least two peer reviewers, you may also receive conflicting advice in your reports. Furthermore, peer reviewers are sometimes guilty of foisting personal preferences on authors as if they are universal rules. It will be your job to reconcile the feedback you get from reviewers and plan how to move forward in consultation with your publisher. Peer reviews are most helpful when you treat them not as the absolute truth about your manuscript but rather as tests of whether your text is working with at least some of your intended readership. Use your peer review reports as a source of clues, if not always direct instructions, about how you can make your manuscript work more effectively.

If and when you receive peer reviews that endorse publication of your book, your acquiring editor will seek approval from their publisher to accept your manuscript for publication. At this point, you'll be asked to lay out a plan for revision in light of the peer reviewer feedback and any additional direction you've received from your publisher. Taking your text through the manuscript development cycle one more time can help you formulate this plan, although you can hold off on executing any edits until you get the go-ahead from your publisher. You'll present your plan in the form of a memorandum of response to the peer reviews, which will be considered by the press's editorial board when they make their decision about whether to put your book under contract.[9] If the publisher approves your editorial plan, your manuscript will be accepted for publication, contingent upon your carrying out the promised revisions.

Moment 3: Development After Approval for Publication

Although approval from the publisher indicates that their staff and editorial board believe your text is essentially publishable, you will likely still be expected to make changes to your manuscript based on the peer reviewer feedback. If you shared an editorial plan in your response memo to the peer reviews, you'll now execute those edits.

Even if your publisher is not requiring major revisions, you may want to rotate through another cycle of manuscript development at this point, reassessing your text while focusing specifically on the needs of your end readers, now that your preliminary readers are all on board. For expert scholars and graduate student researchers, your book needs a well-supported argument that makes a substantial contribution to scholarly knowledge. If you want your book to be useful to instructors and students, your developmental work may be directed at defining specialist terms well enough for understanding by nonexperts and breaking down complex concepts from the scholarly literature. If you hope your book will cross over from academic readerships to other audiences, such as practitioners, policy makers, or activists, your argument needs clear stakes that compel your reader to think or act differently in the real world. For nonacademic readers who read your book out of sheer interest in your subject matter, you'll want to ensure that your structure and style are engaging enough to keep them reading beyond the first page. These are just a handful of ways your developmental work can be affected by your desired end readers. The final round of manuscript development is a good moment to seek feedback from actual members of your ideal readerships so you can learn what they connect with or don't connect with in your current draft and make the needed changes before publication. (For guidance on seeking feedback from various types of readers, see Appendix C.)

How much leeway will you have to make substantial changes to your manuscript after it's approved for publication? In my experience, scholarly book publishers welcome further development of your manuscript when done in service of strengthening the four pillars of argument, evidence, structure, and style. I've worked with many authors who have significantly revised their manuscripts at this stage because they wanted their work to be the best it could be before it reached its end readers. Yet you shouldn't alter the manuscript so much that it becomes a fundamentally different book, because such alterations might require the publisher to reevaluate the project. The book's main argument and contribution should remain true to what the publisher's editorial board has already signed off on, though you may well pursue opportunities to clarify and more strongly present these aspects of your manuscript, especially by improving the book's structure and style. Stay in close contact with your book proposal, your peer review reports, and any correspondence you've had with your editor about your plans to revise.

You might assume that this stage of the publication process will involve close attention to your manuscript from a professional editor at your publisher. You might think that surely someone other than the peer reviewers will read your entire manuscript from start to finish and let you know how it should be improved. You might be hoping for this kind of editorial support particularly if your peer review reports are sparse or vague, or if negative or conflicting criticisms from the reviewers leave you unsure of the best path forward for revision. Many acquiring editors and series editors strive to do a small degree of developmental work, collaborating with authors to push their ideas in promising directions, giving feedback on structure and narrative, and providing guidance on responding to peer reviews. However, the labor conditions of academic publishing are such that editors usually don't have time to give as much attention to each manuscript as they wish to.[10] In most cases, manuscript development will be left almost entirely in your hands. That's what this book will help you with.

You now understand how and when manuscript development figures into the scholarly book publishing process. Extensive lower-level editorial work on your manuscript (e.g., line editing, copyediting, and proofreading) should take place on your very final draft, after peer review and the substantive developmental work is complete. You won't want to invest needless time massaging your prose or correcting typos in parts of the manuscript that might change significantly during your developmental editing. Remember that your manuscript's argument, evidence, structure, and style are the aspects that will make the biggest difference with preliminary readers. If those four pillars aren't strong, it won't matter how polished your prose is or how few typos can be found. Still, you may want to lightly line edit and copyedit your draft each time you send your manuscript to preliminary readers. Such attention will prevent easily avoidable mistakes from interfering with your preliminary readers' appreciation of your ideas and raising questions about your attention to detail. (I discuss post-developmental levels of editing in more depth in Chapter 10.)

My focus in this chapter has been on how the readers you're trying to reach at each stage of the publishing process will affect how you choose to develop your manuscript. In the next chapter I'll discuss other factors that will affect your manuscript development work, such as your professional goals and the time you have available. These factors shape the labor you'll be able and willing to invest in developing your manuscript and should therefore be acknowledged before you go any further into the manuscript development cycle.

Use an Author Questionnaire to Clarify Your Mission in Manuscript Development

Because connecting with readers is the goal of any published work, it's essential to decide who you are writing for so you can develop your manuscript accordingly. The questions that follow will have you record where you are in the publishing process and which readers are of greatest concern at your current moment. The questionnaire will continue in the next chapter to help you further clarify your goals and other factors that will influence your manuscript development. (You can download additional copies of the questionnaire and other materials from this book at manuscriptworks.com/book.)

1. What are the major parameters of your text?
    ◦ The topic: What are you writing about in this manuscript?
    ◦ The scope: Which particular aspects of the topic are you trying to cover?
    ◦ The approach: What kinds of evidence have you gathered to support your claims? Which theoretical framework(s) are you using to analyze your evidence and make your claims? Which scholarly literatures are supporting your inquiry?
    ◦ The overall purpose: What do you want readers to come away from this text understanding, believing, or being able to do after reading it?

Try to answer Question 1 without consulting your text directly as a quick test of whether these major features of the text are even clear to yourself. The topic, scope, approach, and purpose of your manuscript must be clear to publishers so they can determine whether your project is a good fit for their press. Answering these questions without looking at your text can also help you reconnect with your thoughts about the text you really want to write, versus the draft you've managed to produce so far. If you can't readily answer basic questions about topic, scope, approach, and purpose, get these essentials solidified for yourself before proceeding with manuscript development.

2. Which publisher are you working with or planning to submit your project to? Which aspects of your book make it a particularly good fit for that publisher? If you're considering more than one publisher, answer this question for each one.

3. Where are you currently in the publishing process?
   ◦ Moment 1: preparing for initial submission to publishers
   ◦ Moment 2: revising after receiving feedback from preliminary readers but before receiving publication approval
   ◦ Moment 3: preparing the final manuscript to go into production

4. Who are your most relevant readers?
   ◦ Acquiring editors, series editors, and peer reviewers (Moment 1)
   ◦ Acquiring editor, editorial board (Moment 2)
   ◦ End readers (Moment 3)

5. Have you received any feedback from preliminary readers that you intend to consider when developing your manuscript? Summarize the major points.

6. Which end readerships are you hoping your book will connect with? Put a check mark by any that apply. Then rank your readerships numerically to get a clear picture of which one or two audiences are most important to reach.

   _____ expert scholars, including graduate student researchers in your primary field; which field?
   _____ scholars in adjacent fields; which fields?
   _____ undergraduate or graduate students completing coursework

____ readers outside of the academy in professional settings, activist circles, or other communities that matter to you; which readerships?

____ nonacademic readers who have a personal interest in learning about your area of study

2

Delineate Your Goals, Timeline, and Capacity

SCHOLARLY AUTHORS often begin writing their books without taking adequate time to contemplate the work they want those books to do. Maybe the answer seems so obvious that it doesn't feel worthwhile to pose the question. Scholars on the tenure track in "book fields" may find themselves writing a book because that's what people in their position are expected to do. But it's worth pausing to confirm to yourself why you want to publish a book and to recognize that your reasons may have evolved since you started. Knowing your "why" is fundamental, both to keep yourself motivated for the work ahead and to bring a stronger sense of purpose to that work.

It's also important to be aware of any factors that might limit the work you're able to do on your manuscript. You're a whole person and your scholarly production must integrate with the rest of your life, both professional and personal. External forces that pull focus away from your writing are unavoidable, maybe even desirable. Don't set yourself up for frustration by assuming you can and should do everything imaginable to develop your manuscript, because that simply won't be possible for most people. Everyone has limits on their time and energy.

This chapter will help you clarify what you want to do with your manuscript and what resources you have available to do it. In later chapters you'll use this awareness to make a realistic editorial plan.

Clarifying Your Goals

Scholarly authors commonly state these goals as reasons to publish a book:

- securing academic employment
- getting tenure or a promotion
- establishing expertise or burnishing reputation
- participating in scholarly discourse and being cited by other scholars
- having students learn from your research
- shaping public conversations via media coverage or appearances
- influencing policy or professional practice
- engaging with local community conversations
- earning awards and positive reviews
- garnering opportunities such as speaking and consulting gigs, whether paid or unpaid
- generating revenue through book sales (to keep for yourself or donate to worthy causes)
- proving to yourself and others that you can write a book

All these goals are valid. However, it's unrealistic to expect to accomplish all of them with a single book. In fact, publishing a book isn't guaranteed to accomplish any of these goals, except the last one. But awareness of the outcomes you most hope to achieve by publishing a book can help you make more informed decisions about how you write it. You can also be more selective about which feedback and advice to take on as you develop your manuscript, because you can focus on developing your manuscript in ways that will advance the goals with the highest priority.

Many goals are in fact about readerships, because to reach your goals, your book must connect with particular people. Consider again the readerships from Chapter 1:

- expert scholars and graduate student researchers in your field
- scholars in adjacent fields
- undergraduate or graduate students completing coursework
- readers outside of the academy in professional settings, activist circles, or other communities that matter to you
- nonacademic readers who have a personal interest in learning about your area of study

You may even hope that your book will connect with specific individuals, such as mentors, colleagues, funders, or people you discuss in the text itself.

Accept that your one book can't be everything to everyone. A book that's X enough to interest Readership A may not be Y enough to grab Readership B. A position that pleases Reader C may be anathema to Reader D. Getting caught up in satisfying others can lead to a miserable and defensive writing experience, and trying to cater to many different kinds of readers can make your book harder to pitch to publishers. Most scholarly publishers prioritize well-defined scholarly readerships. Your current book isn't the last thing you'll ever write, and you can always present or publish your research in other formats for other audiences if several distinct readerships matter to you.

If you know what you most want your book to do for you, and who you most want it to reach, you can then make intentional decisions about which publisher you want to partner with. You may have to gather more information about publishers before you can make these decisions. For example, if you hope your book will help you get an academic job offer or promotion, find out whether certain publishers are looked upon more favorably by the people who will evaluate your job candidacy or promotion case. Then you may decide to develop your book in certain ways to make it attractive to those publishers. If you want your book to participate in local community conversations, seek a publisher who makes their books affordable to people without access to a university library. If you want to shape professional practice or policy, find out which publishers are most respected in the circles you want to influence. I could go on with additional examples, but you get the picture.

Look at publishing with a particular press as a means to other ends rather than as an end goal in itself. Some press brands carry high levels of prestige or cultural capital, whether broadly or in niche communities. It's fine to want that prestige or cultural capital to carry over to your work, but think about why you want it. Will your book—or your life—be better if you publish with Elite University Press? Not necessarily. Do your research and make sure that any publishers you set your sights on can give you what you need. Discuss your publishing goals with trusted friends, colleagues, and mentors and find out which publishers they recommend. Then, be transparent with publishers about your goals before signing a contract. It's better to know if they aren't the right partner before you get too far down the road.

Once you have a few publishers in mind, familiarize yourself with several recent books they've published that feel comparable to the one you aim to write. What kinds of arguments do these books advance, and how do they position their contributions to their scholarly field or fields? What kinds of evidence and analysis do they present in support of their arguments? How are the books' tables of contents organized and how are the chapters structured internally? How long are the books and their individual chapters? What style are the books written in and how do the authors' voices show up on the pages? You don't have to write your book exactly like these other books—and you shouldn't mimic any of them directly—but understanding what's typical at your preferred presses can help you as you develop your own manuscript.

If you can't identify any publishers that seem equipped to support you in accomplishing your goals, or you're unable to locate multiple comparable titles from the publishers you're considering, expand your search.[1] If the publishers and comparable titles that you find yourself most drawn to aren't scholarly, you'll likely need to take a different approach to developing and pitching your manuscript than what I describe in this book.[2] If you can't find a press that has published the kind of book you want to write, you may need to reevaluate whether your project should be published as a book at all or whether a different form of publication, such as a series of journal articles, blog posts, or podcast episodes, might be more suitable.

Clarifying Your Timeline

The amount of time you have available for developing your manuscript will affect the amount of development you're able to undertake. I'm not referring to an estimate of how much time it would take you to do all the work you want to do. You don't have enough information to make such an estimate, because you haven't yet assessed your manuscript and what its editorial needs are. Instead, calculate the length of time between now and when you must be finished. Accounting for competing demands on your time during that period, figure out how many hours you could realistically spend developing your manuscript, then shape your editorial plans accordingly. If you can't possibly do what must be done in the time available, then you'll need to strategize to extend your timeline or create more time for yourself by sacrificing other activities. But don't worry about that just yet.

The first factor potentially affecting your timeline for manuscript development is the due date set by your publisher. If you're preparing your manuscript for initial submission, you likely don't have any firm deadlines to contend with, but if you've signed an advance contract, your publishing agreement will include a delivery date for your completed manuscript. If you've already been through peer review, your publisher will have a date by which they'll expect your production-ready final draft. Publisher due dates are typically set in consultation with authors, so suggest realistic submission dates when asked. Speak up before signing your contract if you think you'll need more time than what your publisher is proposing. If you've already signed your contract, be aware that publishing deadlines can often be pushed back, unless you're at the production stage, where timelines are more rigid and delays can be costly to the publisher and to you. Setting meetable due dates up front is better than asking for repeated extensions, which could eventually jeopardize the press's commitment to your book.

The second factor shaping your timeline will be your employer's institutional deadlines for reaching certain publishing milestones. This factor may only be applicable if you're on the tenure track and need to publish a book for tenure. Which benchmarks do you need to reach by which dates? Requirements can vary widely from institution to institution, so don't rely on hearsay. Get hard facts, in writing if possible, about what is expected from you. In some cases, a manuscript under contract or accepted for publication will count, whereas in other cases typeset proofs or a physical book must be in hand. Years can pass between signing a contract and having a published book—and some writers never turn in their manuscripts even after signing contracts—which is why some institutions don't consider an advance contract as a meaningful indication that your book will be published. The time from accepted final manuscript to physical book in hand can be a year or more, so understand what your institution expects before calculating when to have your editorial work wrapped up.

Your timeline will also be affected by any external readers you hope to involve in your manuscript development process. If you plan to work with a freelance editor or seek feedback from colleagues or mentors on your manuscript, you'll need to know when those individuals are available and have your manuscript ready for them on time. You'll also need to find out or estimate how long it will take them to turn their feedback around and allow enough time for yourself to incorporate the feedback into your editorial plan before you can move your manuscript along. (I offer additional tips on involving others in your manuscript development in Appendix C.)

Finally, your personal timeline will affect when you need to wrap up your manuscript development. You may have a major life event coming up that you want to be able to enjoy fully without stressing about your book. Acknowledge that your attention and desire to work on your manuscript may have an expiration date and that the developmental work you're willing to undertake will have to fit into a bounded period.

Clarifying Your Capacity

Your overall timeline isn't a span of free time in which you'll have nothing else to do but work on your book. Your capacity for manuscript development during this time will also be affected by competing demands on your mental, physical, and emotional labor. You'll likely have many professional responsibilities in addition to working on your manuscript, such as teaching and service duties if you're employed as university faculty. If you're a scholar from a historically marginalized group, you may find yourself receiving more requests for support from students and more invitations to serve on institutional and external committees. If you work at a teaching-focused institution or in a department with little support for faculty publishing—or if you don't work in an academic role at all—your job may be a significant obstacle to completing your writing and editing.[3]

Beyond work obligations, you might have a variety of other demands on your attention such as caretaking, mental and physical health concerns, financial strain, the need to navigate immigration bureaucracy, stressful national and global events, and other responsibilities that are not necessarily equally or equitably distributed across all scholarly writers. I bring these issues up not to imply that achieving your publishing goals will be more difficult for you than for others, but simply to encourage you to set reasonable expectations for yourself when it comes to determining what you'll be able to accomplish in the time you have.[4]

Before undertaking manuscript development, you may also want to reflect on any internal challenges that could affect the process. If you chronically face perfectionism, anxiety, procrastination, an inability to focus on your writing, the feeling that your ideas aren't worthy of publication, or trauma around previous writing and publishing experiences, it may be worth getting to the bottom of these issues. Internal challenges are structurally conditioned, inequitably distributed, and not to be understood as personal failings. Dealing with emotional blocks around your writing in a proactive way will not only help you feel better in the long-term but will also likely lead to a more enjoyable writing and editing experience when you are able to work on your manuscript.[5]

You're not an inferior scholar if you find yourself with less time and resources to develop your work for publication than you—or others—think you should have. And yet, if you come from a structurally disadvantaged group, professional expectations may, unfairly, be higher for you than they would be for others in terms of your publication output and the perceived rigor of your work. This book will help you to find aspects of your work that you can focus on to get the most mileage out of the time and effort you're able to devote to a writing project, even if you have less capacity than you would wish. Although the method for manuscript development I offer is not a shortcut— you must invest time in implementing it to see results—I aim to help you make the most productive use of the time you have.

Be honest with yourself about your willingness to engage in manuscript development and your desire to publish. Writing and publishing take a lot of work. If your goals can be accomplished by other means, you might decide that developing your text further isn't worthwhile. My suggestions are meant to help you make your manuscript the best it can be, but "best" may not be your goal. Determine what you're willing and able to do under your current circumstances, and perhaps prepare yourself to put your manuscript on hold if you don't have the capacity to develop it right now. This book will be here for you if and when you're able to return to your project.

Use an Author Questionnaire to Clarify Your Mission in Manuscript Development, Part 2

This questionnaire continues from the first part at the end of Chapter 1. Answer these questions based on your current circumstances. Your goals and capacity may shift over time, so take care to revisit these questions each time you rotate through the manuscript development cycle and adjust your answers if necessary. (You can download copies of both parts at manuscriptworks.com/book.)

7. Which goals are you hoping to accomplish through publishing your book? Put a check mark by any that apply. Then rank your goals numerically to get a clearer picture of which one or two goals are most vital to accomplish.

   ____ Securing academic employment

   ____ Getting tenure or a promotion

   ____ Establishing expertise or burnishing reputation

   ____ Participating in scholarly discourse and being cited by other scholars

   ____ Having students learn from your research

   ____ Shaping public conversations via media coverage or appearances

   ____ Influencing policy or professional practice

   ____ Engaging with local community conversations

   ____ Earning awards and positive reviews

   ____ Garnering opportunities such as speaking and consulting gigs

   ____ Generating revenue through book sales

   ____ Proving that you can write a book

8. Which of your intended readerships (see Part 1 of this questionnaire in Chapter 1) are most relevant to accomplishing your top one or two goals?

9. Which publishers are best equipped to help you accomplish your top one or two goals? List any evidence or advice that leads you to believe these publishers will be helpful.

10. What comparable books have been published in the last five years by your top publishers? Try to find two to three books per publisher. Write down each title and anything you want to make note of about each comparable book's argument, evidence, structure, or style.

11. What due dates have been set by your publisher, your institution, external readers, or yourself that you should consider when undertaking manuscript development? How flexible is your timeline if it becomes necessary to extend it?

12. Which other activities are competing for your attention and labor during the time you have available for manuscript development?

13. What internal or structural barriers could impede your manuscript development process? What forms of support can you seek if necessary to increase your capacity to work on your manuscript?

14. Does your project need to be published as a book? What other options exist for accomplishing your goals and reaching your desired audiences? Could any of those options be a better choice for you under your current circumstances?

15. How much work do you want to put into this manuscript right now? It's okay if the honest answer is "as little as possible."

It might feel onerous to record all this information rather than jumping right into assessing your draft. Yet taking time to complete this step could save you from weeks, months, or years of work that wouldn't have brought you closer to your ultimate goals. Once you've clarified the mission of your developmental work, you'll be able to turn to your manuscript with a clearer sense of purpose, a sharper eye for what it needs from you, and a more realistic picture of whether you can give it what it needs in the time you have available.

If your answers to any of the preceding questions cause you to doubt whether you sincerely want to or are able to invest time in developing your manuscript, I encourage you to sit with that doubt. Check back in with yourself after a few days or weeks and see if you're still feeling the same.[6] It's worth doing some soul-searching at this point, because pouring effort into developing a manuscript that's never going to serve your professional aims and personal desires can cost you years of your career and life. But if you are indeed ready to proceed with developing your manuscript, it's time to move on to Phase II: assessing your text.

PHASE II

Assess Your Text

LIKE THE clarifying phase described in the previous two chapters, the assessment phase may be an unfamiliar way of approaching your manuscripts in progress. For many writers, their regular editing process involves diving into their draft on page one and trying to fix problems as they spot them. In contrast, the method described in this book is intended to help you gain a more global view of your manuscript. The method will enable you to diagnose your text's strengths and weaknesses, identify prime opportunities for further development and, most important, equip you to formulate an efficient and effective editorial plan. By identifying opportunities for development—which the next five chapters will help you do—and using your assessment to synthesize an editorial plan before you begin making changes to your manuscript, you can save yourself days, weeks, months, or even years of struggle.

In Phase II of the manuscript development cycle, you're going to read your text with your mind firmly trained on the four pillars that are fundamental to your manuscript's success in the publication process and in connecting with your future readers. As a reminder, these four pillars are **argument, evidence, structure**, and **style**. Your objective will be twofold: to identify opportunities to further develop these aspects of your text and to identify any aspects of your text that are already well developed. In Chapters 4 through 7, I will share the most common opportunities for development of academic manuscripts. But first, Chapter 3 will offer a technique for reading and marking up your text with development in mind.

A quick note before you turn the page: It's normal to feel negative emotions during this phase of manuscript development. You may feel resistance to the new method, shame about the draft you've produced, or overwhelmed about the work ahead of you. If you find yourself feeling discouraged at any point, pause your assessment and turn to "A Few Words of Encouragement" following Chapter 7. Then go back to where you stopped and keep working through the process.

3

Read Your Manuscript
Like an Editor

IF YOU'RE using this book for the first time, I recommend reading this chapter and the following four chapters to familiarize yourself with what you may find when you assess your manuscript. Then return to your draft and use what you've learned to read and critically evaluate your text from beginning to end before proceeding to Phase III.

Marking Up the Text

This procedure will help you shift from the role of author to the role of editor by reading and assessing your manuscript as a developmental editor would. As you read your manuscript, I suggest marking it up in the ways described in this chapter. You can borrow my markup tips or adapt them however you wish. I personally prefer to read and mark up a printed copy of the manuscript, but if you want to mark up the text digitally, that's okay too. Save a clean version of your document before you mark it up, because you'll need that clean version in Phase III. (Appendix B provides a couple sample pages of marked up text.)

As I read the manuscript, I underline anything that feels like an argument or statement of purpose. I put a star by underlined phrases that feel like an especially strong articulation of the book's main thesis or of a chapter's central argument. Not everything that gets underlined gets starred, because stars are reserved for the core claims that drive the entire book or an entire chapter. Differentiating between core arguments and other arguments in this way helps me to see how the various arguments may eventually be nested and prioritized (more details are in Chapter 4).

In the left-hand margin I write the topic of each passage and draw a rectangular box around the topic. I write a new topic and box each time the topic changes, meaning I may end up with multiple boxes next to a particular paragraph or with a lot of space between boxes if a single topic is spanning multiple paragraphs. The spacing between your boxes or repetition of similar topics in different locations can visually alert you to opportunities to improve your manuscript's organization (more details are in Chapter 6).

When I encounter evidence used to support an argument, I write "EV" in the left-hand margin. When I encounter analysis connecting that evidence to the argument, I write "AN." Then I make a bracket to the left of the entire passage so I can see where each piece of evidence and analysis begins and ends.

I circle stylistic issues as I spot them. As you'll see in Chapter 7, only some stylistic issues fall within the scope of manuscript development. Many stylistic issues should be handled during line editing, which comes later (as discussed in Chapter 10). I try to be disciplined about only marking those stylistic issues that represent the writer's overall voice and approach or that directly impinge on other fundamental aspects of the text such as the presentation of the argument. For example, if I see long, convoluted sentences in key places that could interfere with a reader understanding the text's main concepts, I mark those spots, but a random long sentence somewhere else in the manuscript wouldn't concern me at this point. If I see the same type of stylistic issue cropping up repeatedly, I may stop circling it after the first couple instances, because I'll already be aware that it exists and will address it holistically when I make my editorial plan.

I jot notes in the right-hand margin with any immediate thoughts or reactions that come up as I read. If such notes are extensive, I may put them on a separate pad of paper or in a separate document on my computer, always recording the page number that I'm reacting to. I do my best to confine these notes to matters of argument, evidence, structure, and style. Although my notes tend to be about things that need further development, I also call out things that are working well in the current draft. My assessment notes are impressionistic and do not attempt to synthesize or recommend particular editorial interventions. Synthesis and intervention will come later.

Whether you use these markup tips or find your own way of reading to assess your text, the key thing is to conduct your assessment not as your author self but as your newly embodied editor self. Use whatever techniques allow you to stay engaged with reading the text while keeping your mind focused on the four pillars of argument, evidence, structure, and style.

Taking Your Time or Truncating the Assessment Process

Some people will want to assess opportunities to develop their argument, evidence, structure, and style all at the same time. Simultaneous assessment of all four pillars will be easier to do once you're intimately familiar with the common opportunities for development presented in the next four chapters. Other writers may choose to assess their manuscript in four passes, focusing on only one pillar each time. Some may break it down even further, choosing just one or two specific opportunities to look for in each pass. All these approaches are workable.

It's reasonable to go slowly while you're still learning to assess your text in this way. Naturally, the more passes you make through the text the more time assessment may take. Assessment will become more intuitive with practice, and you'll likely feel comfortable taking fewer passes or even marking up and assessing the text all in one pass. If you tackle each pillar separately, I recommend doing so in the order I present them, although you can feel free to find the order that works best for you.

I have just one "rule" for manuscript assessment: Do not edit your text during this phase. I guarantee you'll spot errors and be tempted to quickly fix them, but now is not the time for that. It's too easy to go down a rabbit hole of sentence-level tinkering, when you need to be broadly assessing your text so that in the next phase you can make an overall editorial plan. Editing as you go is inefficient; worse than that, it puts you in a reactive mode with respect to your text. It allows individual issues to distract you from taking in the big picture and making thoughtful decisions about what your manuscript needs. If you feel you simply must make a particular edit as you assess your text, resist the temptation to make alterations to your draft, and instead write a note to yourself about the change in the right-hand margin.

Try not to get frustrated if the assessment process is slow, especially the first few times you go through it. Assessing your text may require many hours over several days. As a professional developmental editor, I would spend ten to twenty hours on this work for a full book manuscript. You may spend less time than I would, because you'll be familiar with the text already.

Or you may spend a little more time than I would if you're still getting the hang of the method. Either way, investing in this process will save you time in the long run because you won't be wasting effort on haphazard revisions. When you're finished, your manuscript will have received the editorial attention it deserves. Over time, you'll gain insight into common patterns in your writing and know which opportunities for development to be on watch for. You will make up time in the next phase by being selective about which opportunities for development you choose to pursue in your editorial plan.

If time is running short, you can truncate the process by setting parameters around the scope of your assessment. When developing your manuscript after peer review, you may choose to focus your assessment on the aspects of your text that were of greatest concern to your peer reviewers. For example, if the reviewers' comments primarily pointed to structural problems, you may want to concentrate on the opportunities to develop your manuscript's structure (Chapter 6) and go into less depth with the other pillars.

If you don't have external feedback yet but you're in a rush to get your manuscript submitted, narrow your assessment to a few specific opportunities, specifically those marked with asterisks in each of the next four chapters. These are the ten most common opportunities for development I've encountered in my authors' manuscripts; the top five are marked with double asterisks. If you're able to develop your manuscript in the top five or ten ways, or even in just a couple, it will likely make a significant difference in the reception of your text. If you find that your manuscript doesn't need further development in the most common areas, you can feel pretty confident that your manuscript is ready for peer review. Further assessment and development can wait until later in the publishing process if you wish.

Opportunities Versus Problems

Throughout the next four chapters, you'll notice that I use the term *opportunity for development* instead of the word *problem*. I do this for a few reasons. First, I'm wary of writing guides that dictate blanket prescriptions for academic texts. Academic writing is shaped by conventions but rarely by strict rules. What someone else might consider a weakness in your text could be a strength in your eyes, something you've done intentionally because you believe it will resonate with the readers you most care about reaching. Furthermore, what's problematic in one discipline may be desirable in another.

In addition, many of the key problems we solve during manuscript development are natural by-products of the scholarly writing process. In fact, some problems aren't problems at all until our goals for the manuscript come into focus during the clarification phase of manuscript development. Clarified goals help us recognize how certain aspects of the text that may have been valuable to the development of earlier drafts are impeding our evolving aims for the final product.

I also prefer the term *opportunity* because it implicitly suggests that you have options. You can choose to pursue any given opportunity—or not. Just because you identify an opportunity to develop your text further in a particular direction doesn't mean that pursuing that opportunity will be the right choice for your manuscript, your publisher, or your goals, timeline, or capacity. Problems demand to be solved, whereas opportunities allow for a more open-ended response.

You have choice in the matter of how you develop your manuscript. If I were to describe all the issues in the next four chapters as "problems," you might assume you need to root out and eliminate all of them to have a chance at publishing your manuscript.

But a decade of scholarly book editing tells me otherwise. Many of the authors I've worked with have garnered publishing contracts and positive peer reviews even while having some of these issues in their texts. Even the most prestigious presses have published illustrious books that contain some of the "problems" I identify in the coming chapters.

I'll share general principles, but you're in the best position to judge what will help your manuscript do the work you want it to do. I want to aid you in making your own decisions about your writing, not tell you what you should or must do according to my preferences. By becoming aware of a variety of opportunities to develop your text, you'll gain the power to explore what your own personal standards are and what you want your finished manuscript to look like.

4

Opportunities to Develop
Your Argument

A NONFICTION book "has to have a reason to exist," says editor Nancy S. Miller, "and it's the editor's job to make sure that reason is evident to the reader on every page."[1] Your book's reason to exist may overlap partially with the reason you're writing it, but not fully. As I discussed in Chapter 2 you may be trying to achieve several instrumental goals with your book. These goals are different from the reason your book exists for your readers.

In scholarly publishing, a book's reason to exist for its readers is sometimes described as its contribution. Your book's contribution is what readers will get in exchange for investing their limited time and attention in reading your book. In a few fields, documenting something's existence and describing it thoroughly could be a strong enough contribution, if enough readers are interested in that. But in most cases, you'll increase the value of your work to scholarly publishers and readers by offering more than documentation. Publishers are looking for an original perspective about your object of study—a core argument—that promises to guide your reader's thinking in a new way. That unique take is what will solidify your scholarly authority and lead readers to use, share, and cite your book, alongside or in place of other books on the same topic.

A scholarly argument is an original claim about your subject that grows out of the research you've done. You'll want your book's core argument to be intriguing enough that readers will be willing to spend a book's worth of time engaging with it, so it shouldn't be too obvious. Scholarly argument also doesn't have to be antagonistic. Although you can test the strength of your argument by asking whether it's a claim that could be agreed with or disagreed with, you may not actually be trying to disagree with anyone. Think of an argument not as an attempt to disagree, but as an attempt to make a point that's intriguing enough that someone would want to read a whole book to learn why it's true.

This chapter will explore several opportunities to develop your book's argument. These opportunities don't exhaust all possible means of developing one's argument, but they do address the most common issues I've encountered. Pursuing any or all of these opportunities will give your book an even more compelling reason to exist, which will significantly increase your manuscript's chances of connecting with publishers and the readers whose thinking you want to shape.[2]

Of the four pillars of scholarly manuscripts—argument, evidence, structure, and style—I start with argument because I've observed a regular pattern in my work as a developmental editor of scholarly books: When the author's argument is clearly established, the rest of the developmental work can usually be carried out straightforwardly. Decisions about which evidence and analysis to include, how to structure the manuscript, and which stylistic choices are appropriate often flow organically from the argument itself.

In the following sections, opportunities marked with a single asterisk are among the top ten most common areas for development I've encountered in scholarly book manuscripts. Opportunities marked with a double asterisk are among the top five. You can find a full checklist of all development opportunities and accompanying assessment questions in Appendix A. The checklist can also be downloaded at https://manuscriptworks .com/book.

Give Your Text an Argument**

It's normal for a scholarly author to not actually know what their book's argument is until after they write a full draft of the manuscript. The authors I work with often conceive their books thinking they want to argue one thing, but after writing everything down, they—or I—realize they're really arguing something else. So don't worry if your book's argument isn't clear yet. That's what manuscript development is for.

If you're not yet sure what argument your text is making, look for clues in the manuscript itself. If you used my techniques for marking up your text (Chapter 3), you'll have underlined many potential arguments and starred the arguments that feel most significant. Consider whether any of those starred passages could become the book's main thesis. If you're still not sure, try writing each underlined argument out on a separate sheet of paper or on individual note cards. Seeing them pulled out of your manuscript may help you identify promising candidates. Play with the order of these arguments to generate ideas about your book's organization. Some arguments may become the main arguments of individual chapters or individual sections within chapters.

If your book is full of description and interpretation but doesn't pull it all together to make an overall point, you may be lacking an argument. Without a driving argument, a series of chapters on a common topic, theme, or research site may not

appear compelling enough in the eyes of publishers and readers. What is the main thing you want your reader to understand
about your topic when they put your book down? That's probably where your true argument lies.

Some manuscripts contain stealthy arguments that hide deep
in the text. If you needed to write 100,000 words to figure out
what you wanted to say, it'd be entirely reasonable if the clearest
statement of your argument were to appear somewhere in the
last chapter of your draft. As you develop your manuscript, you
can now move your argument forward to help your reader understand your text's reason to exist right from the start. If you
articulate your argument as close as possible to the beginning of
your manuscript, you'll inspire your reader to keep reading by
showing that your perspective is of interest to them. You'll also
make it easier for your reader to find, remember, and cite your
argument later on if you locate it within the first few pages.

Assessment questions:

Does the text have a core argument?
Is the core argument stated directly near the beginning of
the text?

A note about the assessment questions:
The questions found at the end of each opportunity
discussion are meant to assist you in deciding which of the
development opportunities you want to pursue. If you worry
that you don't have enough distance from the text to make
accurate assessments, write down your answers to each
assessment question with specific lines from the text that
substantiate your answers. For example, if you answer yes to

Continued on next page

the questions about whether your text has a core argument that is stated directly near the beginning of the text, go ahead and write out your argument in full and indicate which page that statement can be found on. You'll soon realize whether your argument is articulated clearly enough and as close to the beginning of the text as possible.

Distinguish Your Main Argument from Subordinate Arguments and Other Types of Claims*

The length and scope of a book manuscript can lull you into believing that you'll be able to include everything you've ever discovered or thought about your research topic. You've spent so long immersed in your research that you understandably have several arguments or points you want to make. Yet, to make your book's reason to exist cohesive, you'll need to home in on one main point to drive the entire manuscript. You can then consider which of the other points you'll position as sub-arguments to support the driving thesis. These subordinate points will become the main arguments of individual chapters or sections of chapters.

When determining which argument to emphasize as the core thesis of your manuscript, watch out for particular types of claims that authors often confuse with main arguments. These types of claims include premises, implications, exhortations, and what Wendy Belcher calls "claims for significance."[3] A claim based on research others have done or on readily observable facts is more likely to be a premise that sets up your argument rather than an original thesis that could serve as the main argument for your book. A claim that logically follows from another argument in your book, but isn't directly supported by evidence within the text, is probably better thought of as an implication than as a main argument. Premises and implications of your main argument will naturally appear in your book, but be sure to frame them accurately as premises or implications so that readers don't expect to see extensive material devoted to proving them.

Authors also sometimes mistakenly believe that their book should be driven by a normative exhortation. Consider the differences between these two claims:

Claim 1: You should stop doing X because it leads to Y.
Claim 2: Doing X leads to Y because of A, B, and C.

The first claim advances an opinion about a desired course of action, whereas the second claim establishes a truth that is proven by research. The second type of claim is usually more appropriate as the main argument of a scholarly book. The second claim also leaves the reader to decide how they will act on the information conveyed. If you want to advocate for readers to take a particular course of action based on your research, readers will be most amenable to that in the concluding chapter, only after spending the bulk of the book absorbing the scholarly argument and its supporting evidence. Expectations around argumentation vary by field, with authors in some fields being more likely to state a normative position than in others. It may be helpful to consult several comparable books that speak to your intended readership and come to your own decision about what's right for your book.

Claims for significance also don't work as main arguments. Such statements often show up in the form of, "I argue that X is understudied and merits further attention," or "Previous studies have looked at X from Y angle but I argue that we must approach it from Z angle." Those are valid claims, and they may explain your motivations for conducting your research, but they usually aren't the most interesting thing about your project or the most urgent idea you want readers to take away from your book. Your actual main argument is probably about what you found when you paid attention to X or approached it from Z angle.

After identifying the true main argument of your manuscript, you may find that some of the other points you wanted to make don't work as supporting arguments for the main argument. Even if such points are sound and relevant to the topic of the book, they may pull the manuscript in too many different directions. Don't be afraid to cut them loose. Tangential arguments and the evidence that supports them can often be put to good use in other publications. You may be able to generate a whole second book concept or series of journal articles out of your extraneous arguments.

Assessment questions:

If multiple arguments are competing for prominence, which argument is most pivotal?

Can other arguments be nested below the main argument to support it, perhaps as chapter-level or section-level arguments?

Can some arguments be labeled more accurately as premises, implications, exhortations, or claims for significance?

Can some arguments be cut from the manuscript and repurposed elsewhere?

Make Your Argument Portable*

An argument strong enough to sustain an entire scholarly book won't merely state "A is related to B." Instead, it will stake a claim about why or how A has specific effects on B and what the consequences of that relationship are. This kind of argument is stronger because it raises implications that readers can apply in other research contexts. By developing an argument that explains why A has a particular effect on B, you offer your reader a tool that they can use to think about why C has a particular effect on D. Other readers can use your argument to think about the relationship between E and F or G and H. You won't be claiming that the relationship between A and B explains all other possible relationships; rather your argument about A and B will offer readers a new tool to think with and adapt to their own settings. This explanatory tool will thus enable your book to contribute to a broader discourse, beyond the niche conversation taking place among people who care deeply about A and B specifically. Those who study C, D, E, and F can all appreciate your scholarly contribution too. Constructing your argument to be portable in this way can take your book from holding appeal for just dozens of potential readers to being relevant to hundreds or thousands of people in your field and beyond.

One concrete example to illustrate the importance of portability of argument comes from Oliver Haimson, author of the book *Trans Technologies*, published by the MIT Press in 2025. When Dr. Haimson and I worked together on his book proposal several years ago, here's how he articulated his book's argument:

In this book I use qualitative research methods to examine the world of trans technologies: apps, games, digital resources, and other types of technology that help address challenges trans people and communities face in the world, as well as create digital spaces for trans people. I demonstrate that trans technology design processes are often deeply personal, and focus on the technology creator's needs and desires. Thus, trans technology design can be empowering because technology creators have agency to create the tools they need to navigate the world. However, in some cases when trans communities are not involved in design processes, this can lead to overly individualistic design that speaks primarily to more privileged trans people's needs.

This is an outstanding thesis statement because it doesn't stop at making merely descriptive claims about what exists. Haimson doesn't say "trans people design technologies, and in this book I'm going to tell you what they are." That would be an interesting book, but it would primarily interest people who already wanted to read a whole book about transgender tech creators. Haimson goes further by explaining something key about the process of trans technology creation: Creating new technologies can be empowering for trans people because they design from their personal experience and needs and thus develop tools that effectively meet the particular challenges they face. He identifies a cause and effect relationship: Designing from personal experience leads to effective tools. He goes beyond this assertion too, arguing that when designers work in isolation, without involvement from wider communities of trans people, they often end up creating tools that disproportionately benefit individuals most like themselves, who tend to be more privileged than the trans community at large.

Haimson's argument makes for a more portable, more broadly useful book than a book that simply describes several examples of trans technology design. His book will carry value for readers who are interested in processes of technology design in general, even if those readers don't have any prior interest in the particular research focus of trans people or communities. Haimson's book will also be valuable to readers who want to learn about dynamics of privilege and advocacy in marginalized communities, even if those readers have no background in digital technology design. And the book may foster new and productive conversations between those two readerships.

Push your own book's arguments beyond answering "what" questions to also addressing "how" and "why" questions that your evidence and analysis allow you to answer. Don't merely tell your reader what happened in your research. Explain how it happened, why it happened that way, and how it shaped what happened next.

Assessment question:

Is the manuscript's main argument constructed to be portable beyond its immediate research context?

Sharpen Your Argument by Defining Your Main Concepts*

Your manuscript may have a strong, portable argument, but readers will struggle to identify it if it's obscured by imprecisely defined concepts. If you're explaining a relationship between A and B, but you only vaguely sketch what A and B are, readers won't fully appreciate the relationship or why it's significant. This vagueness can cause a well-constructed argument to lose its explanatory power for the reader.

To pursue this development opportunity, find your thesis statement and identify the key terms in it. Then precisely define those terms near the beginning of your text. You can also reinforce your key concepts by naming them explicitly and using consistent vocabulary for them each time they appear throughout the text. Doing so will help to reveal the thread of your argument across the entire manuscript.

> Assessment questions:
>
> Are key concepts defined precisely enough?
> Are key concepts named explicitly throughout the text
> using consistent vocabulary?

Solidify Your Contribution by Aligning the Scope of Your Argument with the Interests of Your Intended Readers

I mentioned earlier in this chapter that the original perspective you bring to your study is your contribution, because it guides the reader to think about the topic of your manuscript in a new way. For your book to have the impact you want it to have among your desired readership, you'll also want to show how that new way of thinking is aligned with ways of thinking that your desired readers appreciate. For example, if you're hoping your book will change how historians think and write about your topic, the crux of your argument should generally be historical. You could cover the same topic for an audience of anthropologists, but for them you'd probably want to frame your argument so that it answers an anthropological question and takes into account previous conversations and theories in that particular field. You'd frame your argument differently still if you were primarily writing for political scientists, literary theorists, or any other readerships that could study the same subject matter.

This development opportunity can be tricky to manage for interdisciplinary scholars, because you may be drawing on conversations and frameworks from several fields. Bringing multiple fields together is fine, and your book may be able to introduce scholars in one field to perspectives from other unfamiliar fields. Drawing on multiple fields is different from contributing to multiple fields, though. Contributing to multiple fields is harder to do successfully, unless you're writing for readers in inherently interdisciplinary fields that are organized more around objects of study than around disciplinary frameworks and methods. For instance, if your book is intended for an interdisciplinary readership in disability studies, your argument will likely feel aligned with your readers' expectations as long as it has something to do with disability. But if you want to make sure that communication scholars in particular take your perspective on board, you'll want to craft your argument so that it touches on specific aspects of disability that are most relevant to communication frameworks, such as how the meaning of disability is constructed or how disability is represented in popular media.

Regardless of what your contribution is, lay it out explicitly somewhere near the beginning of your text. State your argument and explain why it should matter to the people you're writing for. The length of this explanation can vary. In some manuscripts it could be just a few sentences, whereas in others you could spend several paragraphs on it. Consult comparable texts from your field to see how other authors have handled their discussions of contribution.

Early career scholars and scholars who are starting to explore a new research area commonly lack clarity about what their contribution is. Gaining that clarity is part of the process of developing your work for publication, so don't panic if you're still working on it. Get opinions from people who are well versed in the conversations happening in your field. Presenting parts of your work at conferences or publishing portions as journal articles can also be helpful, because you can get feedback from specific audiences and peer reviewers about what they find valuable in your project. Choose your presentation and publication venues carefully to ensure that you're getting this feedback from members of your book's intended readership.

Being the first to study a particular topic is typically an insufficient scholarly contribution in and of itself, because firstness doesn't necessarily correlate with the needs of readers. Your contribution can only hinge on being first if potential readers have been waiting for a book, any book, about your topic. Even if that happens to be true, your case for scholarly contribution will be more convincing if you articulate why a well-defined readership will specifically benefit from your unique perspective and original argument.

Assessment questions:

Is the scope of your main argument aligned with the interests of your intended readership?

Is the manuscript's contribution explicitly articulated?

5

Opportunities to Develop
Your Evidence

IF A core argument is a scholarly text's reason to exist, then the evidence presented in support of that argument is what makes the text viable as scholarship. And if a compelling thesis is one that explains a relationship between entities in a way that can be agreed with or disagreed with, compelling analysis of the presented evidence is what sways the reader to agree with the thesis offered by the author, rather than disagreeing or remaining indifferent. Evidence and analysis are therefore fundamental aspects of your text and must be considered in light of your arguments when assessing your manuscript.

Scholarly readers expect authors to support their arguments with rigorously gathered evidence and sound analysis. What constitutes sufficient evidence and analysis is never a fully settled question, and the concept of rigor has been weaponized by those in positions of power to exclude certain types of knowledge, especially knowledge generated by historically marginalized communities. When assessing whether *your* evidence and analysis are sound enough, you'll therefore want to consider the expectations of your intended readers. Reviewing comparable titles that your desired audiences have received positively is a good way to understand the community standards of evidence and reasoning among the readers you want to connect with.

The goal of this chapter is not to promote allegedly objective or normative standards around acceptable evidence and analysis. Rather, I will help you learn to be more effective at communicating your arguments with well-supported evidence that meets your own community's standards, whatever they may be. I've structured this discussion of evidence, again, around the most common opportunities for development I've encountered in the academic manuscripts I've worked on as a developmental editor. If you choose to pursue some or all these opportunities, your text will become a highly competitive candidate for publication.

As a reminder, you aren't making any edits yet. You're only assessing how your manuscript could benefit from further development in relation to this second pillar. You'll eventually use this assessment to inform your editorial plan, which I'll discuss in Phase III of the manuscript development cycle.

Support All Arguments with Evidence**

If you're like many academic writers, your early drafts may contain some arguments that aren't supported by evidence. This is natural when you're using the writing process to work out your ideas and get your original thoughts down on paper. But once you work out the arguments that will serve as drivers of your book and of its chapters, you'll need to support those points convincingly.

How much evidence you'll need to add will depend on the significance of the claim in relation to the text's overall thesis. For a small, passing point, you may add a single sentence with a quick, concrete example from your research. For an argument that motivates an entire section of a chapter, you may add several lines expanding on something in your research you haven't yet fully explained. A chapter-level argument, that is, a major sub-argument of the book's core thesis, may need multiple paragraphs of evidence.

In some cases, the evidence appears in the text but it's not explicitly tied to the argument it's meant to support, or it may be located too far away from the argument for readers to make the connection. Keep an eye out especially for contextual and background information that's frontloaded in early chapters rather than appearing close to the point it's most relevant to. Editor Melody Herr advises a "just-in-time approach" that distributes essential background information across the text where readers most need it.[1] Moving content within the text becomes a structural matter, so if you're assessing for evidence and structure in two separate passes through the manuscript, make a note to yourself to come back to this issue if necessary.

Assessment questions:

Is each argument in the text directly supported by evidence?

Which arguments, if any, would be more convincing if supported by additional evidence?

Is each piece of evidence explicitly connected to the text's core argument or a sub-argument?

Should any evidence be located closer to the point it's meant to support?

Provide Only As Much Support As Your Arguments Need

Although a lack of explicit connection between evidence and argument is the most common opportunity for developing evidence, I also frequently see authors belabor a fundamental point by offering more stories or data to support it than necessary. You may be tempted to over-support because you've grown attached to certain examples and don't want to leave them out, even if they're bolstering a claim you've already supported well enough. When assessing your text, try to discern whether the collection of evidence you've assembled builds in a compelling way to enhance your argument, or whether it's essentially repeating the same point at the risk of boring your reader. It's easy to fall prey to the sunk cost fallacy, believing that if you've already taken the time to write something into your manuscript, it would be a waste of that time to remove it. As painful as it may be to cut material that you've invested heavily in, it may be a necessary step to keep your text engaging for your reader.

The sunk cost fallacy is even more poignant when a particular piece of evidence took an outsized effort to collect as you conducted your research yet is no longer relevant to your argument as it currently stands. Examples might include a touching story from your fieldwork or a remarkable archival discovery. If the evidence doesn't relate closely to your manuscript's argument, you'll be better off cutting it so that it doesn't detract from the cohesion of your text, although you can hopefully repurpose it for another publication. Or you may have evidence that is genuinely relevant to your argument but takes up too much space or requires more background context than you're able to fit within your target word count. Save such material for a blog post or podcast interview or other venue. If you time the release of this related material to coincide with your book's release, this extra evidence can serve as a preview of your argument for prospective readers, driving them to read your book itself.

In early drafts, academic writers may bring in evidence from other writers' scholarship to support their own arguments. When you're first exploring your research topic, the findings and analyses of other thinkers can help you to form your ideas and situate yourself in an intellectual conversation. It may boost your confidence in your own claims to see that other thinkers have arrived at similar conclusions. However, it's critical to question how much of this material is necessary for your readers, who will likely be coming to your text mainly for your unique viewpoint, as supported by your original research. Once you've collected your own evidence and analyzed it in light of your own argument, you'll likely be able to remove extended discussion of evidence from secondary sources, while appropriately citing the pertinent ideas of other writers. I'll say more about discussions of scholarly literature in Chapter 7, where I address style and balancing your voice with the voices of others.

Do your readers need an extended description of your methods or a defense of your methodological choices in order to find your arguments and evidence convincing? Although you may personally benefit from documenting your methods in detail and being ready to justify them if called upon, your reader likely doesn't want to spend more than a paragraph or two getting acquainted with your methods and methodology. Academic authors tend to over-explain their methods, especially when adapting a book manuscript from a dissertation, a genre in which sustained methodological documentation is in fact appropriate. My usual recommendation is to cut most of the methods discussion, saving the extra material in a separate document. If peer reviewers later suggest more in-depth treatment of methods in the manuscript, you can put the material back in. Extensive discussion of methods may be more appropriate in certain fields than in others, so understanding the disciplinary conventions and expectations of your intended readership is key.

Recognizing that material can be cut from your manuscript is a critical discovery of manuscript development. The possibility of cuts is also a major reason why we do a full assessment and make a strategic editorial plan before executing any changes to the manuscript. You may discover that in fact it's not that the evidence needs to be cut but rather that the argument needs to be reshaped to fit with the evidence you have. For now, you're making note of all potential cuts. When you get to the planning phase you can decide which cuts to make.

Assessment questions:

Is there more than enough evidence to support certain points?

Is there any evidence that doesn't closely support an argument?

Does the text include excessive evidence from the scholarship of other writers?

Does the text include excessive discussion of methods and methodology?

Could any of the excessive evidence be put to use elsewhere?

Present Sufficient and Reasonable
Analysis of All Evidence*

Beyond ensuring that each argument has corresponding evidence in the text to support it, you'll want to ensure that the logical connection between evidence and argument that exists in your head is also adequately explained to your reader on the page. Adequate explanation entails presenting analysis that interprets the meaning of your evidence in light of your argument. Don't assume a connection that's obvious to you will be obvious to readers.

Consider especially carefully the brief story or hook that you may present at the very beginning of your book and possibly at the beginnings of individual chapters or sections. Anecdotes aren't the only possible hooks a writer can use, but they are used so commonly in academic manuscripts that I want to specifically address them here. The purpose of the anecdotal hook is to pique the reader's interest and introduce them to the question that your argument will be answering. However, many writers focus so hard on the first function—capturing the reader's attention with vivid details or an intriguing narrative—that they forget the second function. It's vital to explicitly connect the story that opens your book with the text's main argument. Even a fascinating narrative may not keep an academic reader engaged for long if they fail to see what meaning they should be taking from it. By interpreting your opening hook in light of your argument, you can seize an opportunity to get your main point out there for your reader early on.[2]

Examine all other passages that you've bracketed and labeled EV for evidence. If you haven't yet connected each one to an argument, ask yourself why you decided to include that evidence in the first place. What did you want readers to get out of it? Spell out your answer to this question in the text itself.

Give extra scrutiny to evidence that comes in the form of long quotations from research subjects or from archival material. Long verbatim quotations are sometimes appropriate, but adding your own interpretation will illuminate how the primary source material serves as supporting evidence for your argument. Verbatim quotation is useful when you want to draw your reader's attention to the specific way in which something was originally said. Yet reproducing a lengthy quoted passage is risky, because readers may be tempted to skip ahead to the upshot. This possibility goes directly against your purpose in including the material in the first place. Break up the source material with interpretation and explanation so readers can make a stronger connection with both the material itself and your argument. In some cases, you may decide to forgo direct quotation and convey your interpretation via paraphrasing or interweaving interpretive commentary with your evidence as you present it. Similarly, if your manuscript includes evidence presented in visual form such as photographs, maps, or diagrams, you'll want to incorporate description and analysis of the visual elements into the text itself. Doing so allows you to ensure that readers appreciate the significance they should be gleaning from the image.[3]

Once you've provided analysis for all evidence, double check that your analysis is logically sound. Keep an eye out for potential validity issues, such as inferring intent or feeling on the part of people whose words or actions you're analyzing. Restrict your claims to what you can reasonably conclude from their words or actions rather than making assumptions you can't fully substantiate with the evidence you have access to. If you feel your analytical logic is strong but anticipate that your readers may have objections nonetheless, you may want to acknowledge and address those objections in your text.[4]

Assessment questions:

Does each piece of evidence have corresponding analysis
that connects it to an argument?

Are long passages of primary source material accompanied
by, and possibly interwoven with, original analysis?

Is visual evidence described and interpreted appropriately
in the written text?

Is all analysis in the text logically sound?

6

Opportunities to Develop
Your Structure

STRONG ARGUMENTS and evidence are crucial for a manuscript
to be judged suitable for publication and received positively by
scholarly readers. Yet structure too is fundamental, because a text's
structure is what makes its arguments and evidence discernible
and therefore convincing to the reader. Writers must be intentional about using structure to ensure that readers understand
both what the text's argument and evidence are and how each part
of the text builds logically to the writer's overall point.

A few aspects of structure may merit development in your
manuscript. The first is organization, or how the text orders
component parts to create a sense of logic and narrative flow.
The second is signaling, or how the manuscript intentionally
alerts the reader to the text's underlying organization. Finally,
you'll consider the matter of length, because the need to shorten
or lengthen a manuscript, or any of its component parts, may
have direct consequences for how you decide to structure the
rest of the text.

This chapter is longer than the others in this book. That's pur-
poseful. Academic writers tend to struggle most with structure,

so I want to offer ample support in this area. Structural problems in a text can be among the most difficult and time-consuming to address, but such problems are frequently at the heart of why readers feel a manuscript isn't working. Because structural development can make a drastic difference to the experience of your text for both preliminary and end readers, it's well worth undertaking.

Create a Strong Sense of Narrative with Your Book's Table of Contents**

A scholarly book with a strong sense of narrative begins with an introduction that presents the text's main argument, followed by internally cohesive body chapters. These chapters offer evidence and analysis to support sub-arguments that cumulatively build the book's main argument. The body chapters are ordered with the reader's experience in mind; early chapters might develop the argument in its most straightforward form, whereas later chapters add complexity that takes the argument down new and perhaps unexpected paths. The narrative arc ends by resolving the findings of the research and offering a direction for the reader to go after finishing the text.

Narrative in scholarly writing doesn't necessarily translate to a literal story that starts at the beginning of the text and continues all the way through, featuring the same people and places in every chapter. Scholarly narrative can be a more abstract story of your thinking or of a particular conceptual problem that can be traced through various sites or historical moments. In expository texts, "the 'protagonist' is an idea and the 'plot' a series of supporting arguments through which that idea must pass, like a classic hero whose journey is marked by tests of strength and wit," suggests editor Scott Norton.[1] Whatever the narrative arc of your manuscript is, readers will find the text more rewarding to engage with if a palpable logic drives the order in which the material is presented.

If your manuscript presently lacks an underlying logic, it doesn't mean you're a bad writer. It merely means that you've been using the writing process to work out your own thinking. Your focus has rightly been on getting your thoughts expressed in an external form or even figuring out what your thoughts are. Now that you've proceeded from drafting to development, it's time to arrange those thoughts in an order that assists your reader in following your thinking. Making your manuscript work for readers is the goal of manuscript development, so if you're just now thinking about how to better organize your text, you're right where you need to be.

The first step in assessing your text's organization is to obtain a clear view of how it's currently arranged. You'll need this organizational view both at the highest level of your book's chapter structure and at lower levels, drilling down to sections within chapters and paragraphs within sections. If you've already written an annotated table of contents, perhaps as part of your book proposal, you have a head start.[2] If not, draft one now. Make a five-column chart on a pad of paper, in a blank document, or in a spreadsheet, with the following headings at the top of the five columns:

1. Page range
2. Topic of the chapter
3. Purpose of the chapter
4. Location logic
5. Editorial ideas

Each row of the chart will correspond to one chapter. In the topic column, use chapter titles if your current titles are descriptive enough. The purpose of most body chapters is to advance a chapter-level argument that supports the book's main argument, so in the purpose column, state the chapter-level argument and how it supports the book's main argument. If the chapter isn't a body chapter, its purpose might be to introduce the book's topic and argument, to conclude the narrative, to provide optional information for the reader, or something else. In the location logic column, explain why the chapter appears in this spot in the table of contents. If the chapter is first or last, why does it belong in that position? If the chapter appears somewhere in the middle, how does the chapter relate to the chapters that appear before and after it? In the editorial ideas column, record any thoughts you have about reorganizing your material at the chapter level (see Appendix B for an example of this chart filled in).

If you haven't yet thought about why you've arranged your chapters in the order you have, the five-column chart will stimulate your thinking about that and help you verbalize how the material in your book is demarcated and related in a cohesive way. If your current chapter-level organization isn't yet logical or cohesive, this exercise will reveal it. If you make your chart on physical paper, you can cut the rows into individual strips and play around with rearranging them until you find an order that works.

During manuscript development, the chapter-level structure may be in flux for quite a while. As you continue your assessment, you may find that some material needs to be moved from one existing chapter to another. You may also need to deconstruct a few chapters and rebuild them in a new arrangement of the material. You may find that it makes sense to radically reconceive your entire table of contents, as you clarify your argument for yourself. This potential for the chapter structure to change is one reason why it's so important to fully assess your manuscript before attempting to execute edits sequentially within individual chapters.

The next development opportunity is to look critically at the way your material is organized at the level of sections and paragraphs, which may also prompt new ideas about how to better organize it at the chapter level.[3]

Assessment questions:

Is there an underlying narrative logic to the order of your chapters?

Would this narrative logic be clear to readers?

Does each chapter have its own cohesive argument or purpose in relation to the entire text?

Organize Your Material in a Logical Flow at the Section and Paragraph Level*

Setting aside your tentative table of contents for a moment, explore how the pieces of your manuscript fit or don't yet fit together at the section and paragraph levels. If you've already marked up your manuscript as suggested in Chapter 3, you've already taken your first step toward assessing your text's organizational logic by marking each topic as it appears in the text. Taking time to make these topical notes can alert you to certain organizational problems, such as packing several topics into one paragraph or section without fully developing the points you want to make about each topic. Or you may become aware that you keep returning to the same topic in various places, causing your text's narrative to feel overly repetitive.

If you suspect organizational problems but aren't yet sure how to fix them, build on your topical markup. Open a fresh pad of paper, blank document, or spreadsheet, and list all the topics in order along with the page numbers where they can be found in the current draft. This kind of list is sometimes called a reverse outline. Seeing all your topics listed separately from the text can spark ideas about reorganization. Then make notes about how you think certain passages might be relocated or rearranged to achieve a more logical flow. I like to write these notes in a different color ink directly on my topic list.

If necessary, you can go even deeper with your list of topics to produce an outline of the organizational logic of your text. To create this outline, make a five-column chart similar to the one you made for your annotated table of contents. Give this chart the following headings across the top from left to right:

1. Page number or page range
2. Topic of the passage
3. Purpose of the passage
4. Location logic
5. Editorial ideas

Fill in the chart, topic by topic, from start to finish as you go through a given section of your text. The entries in column one will always be in consecutive order as you move through the pages of the manuscript. In column two, transcribe the topic labels from your markup. In column three, note why you've chosen to discuss the topic of the passage and the key point you want readers to understand from the discussion. In column four, articulate why you've chosen to discuss the topic at that particular spot in the text. If your location logic is sound, no changes may be needed. If reorganization is indicated, jot thoughts in column five about where the passage might move to, whether it should be combined with other passages, or whether it should be removed from the text altogether. You might draw arrows between rows of your chart or use other symbols to indicate moves. You could also cut your chart into strips and rearrange the rows physically to see if that helps you arrive at a better order for the material[4] (see Appendix B for an example of this chart filled in).

Undertaking this kind of structural assessment using the five-column outline can be time-consuming and mentally taxing. I recommend using this technique only on limited portions of your manuscript where you are struggling the most with organization. Start with the first two columns and fill in more detail only as needed. Particularly thorny sections may require the full treatment, but simply starting the process will likely help you work out many organizational problems that seemed intractable at first.

If your structural assessment shows that parts of your manuscript need to be disassembled and reassembled from the ground up, you may find it helpful to think about your chapters and sections within chapters as shorter argumentative essays containing their own introductions, evidence, analysis, and conclusions. Zachary Schrag, author of *The Princeton Guide to Historical Research*, suggests that almost all historical writing can be scaled up or down from the "foundational five paragraph essay." As Schrag acknowledges, the actual number of paragraphs in each "essay" need not equal five, and the length of each part can vary depending on the amount of introductory context and supporting evidence needed for each component argument.[5]

As a developmental editor of scholarly monographs across varied academic disciplines, I've found that nearly all book chapters can be productively structured as Schrag suggests. Most chapters consist of an introduction, conclusion, and three to five supporting sections in between, each of which has its own internal intro–support–conclusion structure. I never impose the number of internal sections in a chapter a priori, but the appropriate number almost always ends up falling in that range. This tip isn't meant to reduce your chapters and chapter sections to a series of simplistic templates. Rather, the five-paragraph essay concept helps writers to see how their long and complex manuscripts are really composed of manageable pieces that can be edited and moved around in chunks if necessary.

Assessment questions:

Does each piece of material have a purpose that serves the chapter's argument and the manuscript's overall argument?

Does the order of your material help pull your reader through the logic of your text at the section and paragraph level?

Consider Conventions When Deciding How to Organize Your Book into Parts

As you think about organizing your material into chapters, sections, and paragraphs, be aware of genre conventions around such organizational units. Scholarly publishers and readers generally expect each body chapter of a book to be a self-contained unit, animated by a cohesive topic, set of evidence, and sub-argument that supports the book's main thesis. In addition, readers will expect the order of the chapters to be well-conceived and dictated by the overall argument of the book, with each chapter building upon what came before and deepening the book's contribution.

Other chapter types have their own genre conventions as well, and understanding these conventions will help you assess where certain kinds of material should appear. Introductions engage the reader's attention and familiarize them with the book's overall argument and contribution, giving the reader a reason to keep going with the rest of the book. An introduction chapter also provides the reader with the context to understand what follows.[6] A preface comes before the introduction and is typically written in a more personal mode, often discussing how or why the book was written, although some authors will incorporate such discussions into the introduction instead. Conclusions may be approached in various ways, but they often sum up the text's biggest implications and suggest next steps for the reader to take, including new lines of research to pursue. For the most part, readers expect introductions and conclusions to frame and support the material that comes between them. This expectation is why I warn writers against presenting significant evidence in a book's conclusion. By that point in the text, readers expect to be winding down and reflecting back, not integrating new substantive information and aspects of the argument. Appendixes appear in the back matter of the book and house relevant information that isn't essential to the book's main narrative but that may nonetheless be useful to many readers, particularly those who take a more specialist interest in the book's topic or methods.[7]

You may have reasons for wanting to depart from generic conventions. Such departures can work because these are norms, not absolute laws. Bear in mind that your readers—including preliminary readers such as peer reviewers—may have a smoother experience of your text if you adhere to convention. Scholarly readers are more likely to trust you as an authority in your field if your text follows the "recognized forms" that your research community "uses to represent not just *what* it knows but also *how* it knows."[8] If an unconventional structure is integral to your argument, or you have another reason to upend reader expectations, make sure your justification for changing it up is self-evident within the text. Your text's underlying organizational logic must be particularly clear if you're asking readers to parse an unfamiliar structure while also processing the new information you're presenting.

> Assessment Questions:
>
> Do your body chapters function as self-contained units with their own cohesive topics, evidence, and sub-arguments?
>
> Do your other chapter types also adhere to genre expectations for scholarly books?
>
> If you said no to either of the preceding questions, do you have well-considered reasons for departing from convention, and will those be clear to the reader?

Use Titles, Headings, and Topic Sentences to Signal Content and Purpose to the Reader**

You can use structural cues to reinforce the narrative logic of your manuscript, once the material is organized as you want it to be. Structural signals in the text begin with the main title, which is likely the first thing a potential reader will see. The reader may use the title to decide whether they want to engage with your scholarship at all. If they decide to engage, they'll then consider your chapter titles, and as they begin reading, they'll be guided through the chapters by your section headings.

Well-crafted titles and headings prepare the reader to learn something significant about the subject being covered. Titles and headings are most effective when they both indicate the topic of the upcoming material and orient the reader toward the point the writer wants to make about the topic. Take the heading of the section you're reading right now as an example. I could have used the heading "Titles, Headings, and Topic Sentences" because that's ostensibly the focus of this set of paragraphs. But by using the heading "Use Titles, Headings, and Topic Sentences to Signal Content and Purpose to the Reader," I've tried to convey why you should care about titles, headings, and topic sentences when assessing your manuscript. The heading has given you a reason to read this section, or it might've helped you navigate the text by letting you decide to skip this section.

Topic sentences function in an analogous way to titles and headings, helping readers to traverse the contents of smaller passages and individual paragraphs. These sentences appear at or near the beginning of a section or paragraph, letting the reader know what they'll be reading about in the next several sentences. The most effective topic sentences, like the most effective titles and headings, also clue the reader in to the point they will be taking away by the end of the passage. The topic sentence of the paragraph you're currently reading indicates that topic sentences are useful in communicating with readers and suggests that the rest of the paragraph will be dedicated to explaining how. Like titles and headings, topic sentences prepare the reader to care about the content that follows, again by establishing that the content is significant in some way that matters to the reader.

Beyond their function in engaging a reader's interest and preparing them for the material to come, well-crafted titles, headings, and topic sentences collectively paint a coherent picture of how the entire text will unfold. A thoughtfully constructed table of contents can stand alone as an elegant snapshot of your book's entire argument, allowing your reader to glean the intellectual contribution of your work before they even read it. Although your readers may never see your text's headings or topic sentences presented together as they do the chapter titles, a reader who is skimming your text quickly could hypothetically grasp your contribution by looking only at headings and topic sentences. Of course you'd like readers to engage deeply with your book, but if they were able to process, absorb, and share your main points with others based on skimming alone, that would still be a pretty good outcome.

Titles, headings, and topic sentences are all sometimes categorized under the term *signposting*. Writers receive feedback that their text needs more signposting when the significance of the parts and the relationships of those parts to each other aren't clear to readers. Reviewers also call for signposting when confusing jumps between sections cause the sequence of material to appear random rather than intentional. However, adding signposts that merely announce or list what's coming up won't fix the true problem, because such signposts don't remedy the fact that the structure doesn't support the argument in a logical way.

When the writer arranges the content logically so that readers are organically pulled along through each step of the underlying argument, explicit explanations of the text's organization are less necessary and reviewers are less likely to request more signposting. Furthermore, when you organize your text thoughtfully and then signal that organization, it takes a burden off your reader. Your reader will be better able to engage with your text's content because they'll understand how each piece fits into an overall purpose without having to stop and figure it out for themselves.[9]

To assess the effectiveness of your titles, headings, and topic sentences, begin by noting whether they exist at all. If you've been using nondescript placeholders, such as "Introduction" or "Chapter 5," or beginning new sections with line breaks or abstract symbols, coming up with new titles and headings will be an important part of your editorial plan. If titles and headings are in place, you can test whether they're effective by creating an outline of your text consisting only of the titles and headings that currently exist. Take your outline down to the level of topic sentences if you want to test those too. Does your outline produce an accurate map of your text, including your argument, sub-arguments, and all the evidence you use to support them?

Useful titles, headings, and topic sentences are often lurking in your text already, even if they're not currently located at the beginning of the passage they apply to. Because you've used the initial drafting process to figure out what you think and ultimately what you want to convey to your reader, the best articulation of your complete thought might naturally emerge at the end of an early draft. During assessment, you can find these statements of purpose and make a note that they should be promoted to title, heading, or topic sentence position, where they can frame the material that follows. If you can't find these statements already buried in your text, you may be able to find them in your five-column outline. If you haven't made a five-column outline yet, try it only for the passages that still need good headings and topic sentences.[10]

You may privately feel that your text is organized with such impeccable logic that it doesn't need overt signaling, but I would be suspicious of the idea that you have no need to clue your reader in. It's worth taking time to craft illuminating titles, headings, and topic sentences before sending your manuscript to preliminary readers. Norms around the use of headings in particular can vary by field. Consulting comparable books aimed at your intended readership can give you a sense of what's expected. But regardless of what the norms are, if you're receiving feedback from preliminary readers that the purpose of a particular chapter, section, or paragraph is unclear—or if preliminary readers explicitly call for more signposting—consider whether you could be using titles, headings, and topic sentences more effectively to reveal the underlying logic you had in mind.[11]

Assessment questions:

Do all units have descriptive titles, headings, or topic sentences?

Does the text's main title and subtitle clearly convey the topic of your manuscript as well as hint at your approach to the topic?

Does each chapter title clearly convey the topic and approach of the chapter?

Does each section heading clearly convey the topic and approach of the section?

Do you use topic sentences effectively throughout the text?

Use Breaks and Transitions to Signal Relationships Between Parts of the Text

Whereas titles, headings, and topic sentences orient the reader to upcoming material, breaks and transitional language help readers understand how parts of the text relate to each other. Breaks between sentences, paragraphs, sections, and chapters implicitly reveal that one complete idea or line of argument has been wrapped up and a new one is being broached.

When assessing whether your breaks are working effectively, look for whether the breaks align with the conceptual demarcations that exist in your head. You may also need to insert breaks where none exist yet. For example, if your topic markup exposed that you were trying to cover multiple topics in a single paragraph, you'll want to insert paragraph breaks between the topics, then fully develop one idea about each topic within its own paragraph. Breaks may be dictated not only by shifts in topic but also by shifts in purpose. You may divide a section into smaller sections with their own designated purposes, or you may merge sections that are essentially making the same sub-argument. Column three of your five-column outline can help you detect where such breaks belong.

While breaks implicitly signal to a reader that the two units on either side should be understood as different in some way, transitional language explicitly signals how the two units on either side of a break relate to each other within the logic of the text. Explicitly transitional language is helpful when you want the reader to understand a relationship that's more nuanced than "these are two separate ideas." An effective transition can help your reader understand that the second idea builds on the first to reinforce it, or that it exposes something significant in contrast with the first, or that it takes the argument in a new direction, to give just a few examples.

Transitional language might be incorporated into headings and topic sentences or deployed at the end of a unit to set up the next one. Wherever transitions appear, they are most effective when they communicate the logical *relationship* between the parts. This is why transitions and topic sentences that merely announce the topic of the upcoming passage are so ineffective, even becoming tiresome to readers. Had I begun this section of my book with a statement such as, "Having just discussed titles, headings, and topic sentences, I will now discuss breaks and transitions," I would have been telling you something you'd soon discover anyway. The actual transition sentence at the beginning of this section was more effective at communicating that the two sets of signaling tools perform related but distinct functions in the structure of a manuscript.[12]

Assessment questions:

Do breaks in your manuscript between chapters, sections, and paragraphs accurately signal shifts in topic or purpose?

Do you use transitional language to illuminate the relationship between material on either side of major breaks in the text?

Shorten or Lengthen Your Text to Align with Reader Needs and Publisher Requirements

The length of your manuscript will naturally fluctuate as you pursue various opportunities to develop your argument and evidence. If you decide that certain lines of argument are not closely related to the main thesis, you'll cut that material from the manuscript, reducing length. If you decide that a point needs additional evidence to adequately support it, your manuscript will get longer. In an ideal world, the length of your manuscript would be organically determined by the points you were trying to make and whatever evidence was needed to back up those points. However, in the real world, publishers are working within constraints on production and distribution that limit the acceptable length range for book manuscripts. To get the length right, you thus need to return to your mission in terms of your publication goals and intended readership (Chapter 1). Compare recently published books by authors who are at a similar career stage and are writing for similar audiences to determine what the acceptable ranges for total length and chapter length might be for you.

To assess whether your manuscript and chapters are the right lengths, simply check the word counts in your current draft and see if increases or decreases are needed to bring your manuscript's length in line with general norms or your publisher's requirements. For scholarly monographs in most fields, publishers typically prefer total word counts that range from 70,000 to 100,000 words. Averages vary by discipline, with books in the sciences and social sciences falling at the lower end of the range. Books in the humanities and other fields that use extensive primary source documentation, such as legal studies, tend to fall at the higher end. An edited anthology might be quite a bit longer than 100,000 words, whereas a short guide intended to provide an introductory overview of a timely topic might run just 30,000 to 40,000 words. Total word counts always include notes, bibliography, and any ancillary material such as appendixes and acknowledgments, though not indexes. Book chapters commonly range from 5,000 to 15,000 words, again varying by discipline and intended readership.

Publishers and readers will also have expectations about the relative lengths of component parts of a manuscript. The general expectation is that chapters will be roughly equal in length, though introduction and conclusion chapters may be shorter than body chapters, which present evidence and novel developments of the argument. Unequal chapter lengths are often symptomatic of other problems with a manuscript, such as a bloated chapter-level argument that should be split up into multiple chapters and sub-arguments, or a particularly short chapter whose argument needs far more supporting evidence to make its point convincingly. In those cases, the chapters usually end up more equal in length after completing developmental work on argument and evidence. However, if you have thoughtful reasons for some components of your book being shorter or longer than others, or if your entire manuscript departs from length norms, there may be wiggle room with your publisher. Make certain that your justification for defying expectations makes sense in the context of the work's purpose and intended readership, and be prepared to explain your choices in your book proposal and perhaps in response to peer reviews if concerns are raised.

If you find during structural assessment that your manuscript or any of its components is significantly longer than it should be, the most efficient remedy is to identify the largest viable unit that can be removed wholesale. If your book is over ten thousand words beyond the ideal length, look for an entire chapter that can be cut and ideally repurposed as a separate publication. If a specific chapter is too long, look for several paragraphs or a whole section that can be removed. To determine which chunks can go, return to the driving purpose of the larger unit, whether book, chapter, or section within a chapter, and cut supporting material that isn't strictly necessary. If everything currently in the unit falls within the scope of the unit's argument, consider whether you could curtail the scope of this unit's argument, allowing you to adequately support it in the space that you have available.

The alternative to removing the largest viable unit is to chisel away at smaller units of the text, removing paragraphs, sentences, and even individual words that aren't necessary to the reader's understanding of the text. This approach can work if you want to remove a few thousand words or less, but it will involve many more editorial decisions, and each cut will likely necessitate more time and effort to adjust the text that remains.

I would only attempt the chiseling strategy if the largest-viable-unit approach proved unfruitful. There may be other good reasons to tighten up your text at the paragraph and sentence level, but if you're not doing so with the express purpose of reducing length, you can handle such tightening during line editing after your developmental edits are complete.[13]

If the problem at hand is that a book, chapter, or section isn't long enough—a rare problem with academic writers in my experience—then brainstorm additional layers of the argument that could generate new material. Look at holes you've identified in the current draft, in terms of argument or evidence, or consider questions you've raised but not yet answered. How much length might be added by filling those holes or answering those questions, and how close will that get you to the target length for your manuscript?

Assessment questions:

Is the total length of your manuscript on target for your intended publisher or norms in your field?

Are your chapter lengths consistent with norms in your field?

Are the lengths of component parts, such as chapters and sections within chapters, roughly equal to each other?

If you answered no to any of the preceding questions, do you have reasonable justification for departing from convention?

7

Opportunities to Develop
Your Style

STYLE IS the final pillar to be considered in your developmental assessment. The style of your manuscript encompasses certain general decisions you've made about how to present the material, as well as how your voice comes across in the text. An engaging style will help you build a stronger connection with your readers. It can make the difference between a reader grudgingly skimming for needed nuggets of information or eagerly reading your book from cover to cover. Your writing style should project commitment to your claims and conclusions, which helps your readers easily comprehend what you're trying to do with your work and accept your authority to do it.

Some matters of style are appropriate to address during developmental editing, whereas other stylistic matters are better dealt with in a later stage of manuscript preparation, such as line editing or copyediting. In this chapter, the focus is on stylistic choices that apply to your entire text and could meaningfully affect your reader's ability to grasp your argument and contribution. Matters of diction, syntax, and grammatical correctness will thus not be our main concern at this time. I recommend assessing and editing your text for these matters only after your developmental revisions are complete (see Chapter 10). I encourage finer editing during the developmental phase only when sentence-level obfuscations could interfere with your reader's grasp of the main points you're trying to get across. Such issues will be addressed later in this chapter.

What is stereotyped as a lack of style in academic writing is actually a particular style in itself, one that is perpetuated by the scholarly habitus. Certain writers are held up as great thinkers during graduate school training, and you may have been led to believe, if only implicitly, that you must write like them if you want to be taken seriously. This belief isn't necessarily wrong, because academic gatekeepers do sometimes seize on writing that doesn't fit the traditional stylistic mold—which in many disciplines is heavily biased toward Western, white, masculine, upper-class, straight, neurotypical norms—and actively attempt to exclude scholars who depart from that paradigm. Real risks face an author who wants to develop a distinctive voice and make stylistic choices that might be viewed as unconventional by those in positions of power.[1]

In light of these risks, any developmental work you do regarding matters of style must be especially attentive to the context in which you're working, who you're prioritizing as readers, and what your goals are for your manuscript (as discussed in Phase I). As in previous chapters, this discussion is structured around the development opportunities I've most frequently encountered in my work with academic authors. The principles I share in this chapter aren't universal rules. Pay attention to how stylistic matters are handled in the comparable books you've collected to serve as inspirations for your text. As always, decide for yourself whether to pursue any of these development opportunities in your own manuscript. My only prescriptive advice is to be intentional and consistent about your stylistic choices, whatever they may be, so that you can justify them if called upon to do so.

Foreground Your Own Ideas**

Because most scholarly writing is meant to contribute to an ongoing intellectual conversation, you'll naturally want to include the ideas of other scholars in your text. Your contribution can only be recognized as a contribution in the context of what others have previously thought and written, which means you will sometimes have to explicitly discuss other scholarly texts. Quote and cite other scholars to give due credit to the ideas that have influenced you, especially when you've learned from thinkers who are too often marginalized in scholarly discourse.

However, it takes work to get the balance right between your voice and the voices of others. It's incredibly easy to allow the ideas of other thinkers to occlude your own original thoughts in early drafts. This phenomenon is understandable for writers who are just beginning their scholarly careers and still figuring out where their ideas fit into their fields. Excessive discussion of secondary sources is also common for more experienced authors who are writing about a new topic and attempting to find their footing in a particular scholarly conversation. Indeed, although over-discussion of the literature is widely associated with books based on dissertations, the issue can be equally prevalent in manuscripts written by senior scholars.

When developing your manuscript, remember that readers will be spending time with your book because they care about, or are prepared to care about, what you in particular have to say.

Therefore, you'll serve your reader most effectively by fore-grounding your original argument and bringing in others' words and ideas sparingly as supportive background. Long summaries of other scholarship—let alone long block quotations of secondary sources—are not what your readers are coming to your book for. Don't let your reader forget that you are not only participating in a conversation but also adding something essential to it. Your addition will be what gives readers the motivation to engage with your work.

You can respectfully acknowledge the work of others while keeping your own voice and contribution present. One way to do this is to gloss other scholarship in your own words wherever possible. In doing so, you can still cite and even directly quote key terms and concepts while ensuring that no one else's words are taking up more space than your own. Where you feel it necessary to quote another thinker at length, interweave their words with your own interpretation, bringing the focus back to what your readers are supposed to be understanding about the quoted material in light of the point you are making.[2] Keep an eye on topic sentences in particular to make sure your ideas are framing the paragraphs you write, even if you summarize the ideas of others within those paragraphs.

As you assess your manuscript, you may realize that some of the citation and summarization of others scholars' work is only loosely connected to any of the original points you want to convey to your reader. Some discussions of the literature may be there because they were important to you at a previous stage in the development of your thinking about your topic. Now, discern whether each of those references remains important to your reader's understanding. In many cases, you'll be able to trim down or eliminate such material, now that your thinking has solidified.[3]

Assessment questions:

Do the words of others take up more space than your own
in any given paragraph or section of your manuscript?
When discussing the ideas of other scholars, do you always
make clear how they connect to your own points?
Are there any references to other scholarship that are no
longer necessary to include?

Make Considered Choices About Notes

Notes are a hallmark of scholarly manuscripts. Scholars use notes
for a number of reasons: to cite related scholarship; to document where or how they found a piece of evidence; to explain
something that certain readers might want more information
about or point to sources where such explanation can be found;
to pursue supplemental lines of argument; and—let's be
honest—to share random factoids or humorous asides that they
couldn't figure out how to integrate into the main text.

Nothing provokes defensive response among scholarly writers
like telling them how they should handle their notes. Although I
have my own opinions about how notes are best used, I'm not
here to impose my thoughts on you. Instead, choose a coherent
approach to your notes that genuinely considers what will be
helpful to your reader. Establish which functions you'll use notes
for, and decide whether any of the material currently in your
notes should be integrated into the main text. Understand how
notes are used to perform authority in your particular field, and
determine what's appropriate in light of your goals for the manuscript. As always, consult some comps to see what the norms and
feasible departures are. If you make the stylistic choice to include

extensive notes, it should be an informed choice with a justifiable purpose. Unfortunately, "I couldn't figure out how to fit this in the main text" is not a justifiable purpose.

Your approach to notes also includes the decision whether to use footnotes that appear on the main pages of the text or endnotes sequenced at the end of the manuscript. The choice between footnotes and endnotes is often not the author's to make, although you may be able to express a preference to your publisher. If you do have a preferred location for notes, be prepared to explain why your choice will serve your readers best.

Assessment questions:

Do you take a coherent approach to notes across your manuscript?
If you make extensive use of notes, is such an approach necessary or advantageous in your field?

Strike a Consistent and Appropriate Tone

Tone is the way you use words and phrases to express your attitude toward the subject matter you're writing about and toward your reader. Tone can place you at a distance from both subject and reader, or it can bring you emotionally or politically close to subject or reader. Both distance and closeness can be ways of establishing your authority and winning your reader's trust, depending on your audience. Rather than assuming that all scholarly writing must be objective—or that all scholarly writers should attempt to perform objectivity by concealing their subjectivity—consider who your readers are and how you can connect with them most effectively.

Many scholarly fields recognize that all writers bring ideological and personal commitments to their texts. Most of the authors I work with are situated in such fields, and their commitments are what drive their work and provide the impetus for wanting to publish in the first place. Still, certain tonal conventions may be expected by academic readers, so consider how breaking with convention might affect the impact of your text on the readers you want to reach. If you appear to be judgmental or dismissive about the thoughts or behaviors of your readers, or of the people you're writing about, you may jeopardize your reader's willingness to trust you. Offering praise or admiration for your research subject that is unsupported by critical analysis may cause your reader to wonder whether you've included all the relevant information they need to draw their own conclusions. As the writer of a scholarly book, you'll want your readers to recognize that your points are substantiated by solid research and analysis rather than mere opinion.

The emotions you feel as you write about your topic will naturally show up in the tone of your text, especially in early drafts. You might feel angry about an injustice you've studied. You might feel defensive about criticism you've received in the past. You might feel frustrated at people in your field who disagree with your claims or are indifferent to the questions that matter to you. The manuscript development phase is when you get to decide whether and to what extent you want these emotions to come across in your published writing. Again, consider your goals in publishing a book and what is most likely to resonate with your intended readers.

The level of formality or informality in your writing is also part of your authorial tone. Different levels of formality will be appropriate depending on your intended publication venue and readership, so I won't make any prescriptions about formal language here or say that informality is always bad in scholarly writing. The key questions are: Is the level of formality consistent throughout the manuscript, and is it suited to your publication context?

If formality is appropriate for your intended publisher and readers, it doesn't mean your text has to be dry or boring. Consider how you might incorporate lively description of the people, places, and things you encountered in your research to set the scene for your findings. Such concrete language is "the stylish writer's magic bullet," which can allow your words to "engage the senses and anchor your ideas in physical space," says writing expert Helen Sword.[4]

Blake Atwood provides an example of concrete description from his scholarly book called *Underground: The Secret Life of Videocassettes in Iran*:

> Hamid waited patiently while the agents shuffled through his papers. Jeans, a t-shirt, and slicked-back hair showcased his sharp 1980s style but also quietly revealed his profession. It was 1987 and Hamid had just left war-torn Iran. Hoping to emigrate to the United States, he landed in Ankara, Turkey, where he had arranged for a visa interview at the American Embassy. As they dug through the details of his personal life, officials asked Hamid about his line of work. "I am an underground video dealer," he said cautiously. Worried his candor would ruin his chances of getting a visa but also afraid to lie, he braced himself for the worst. Instead the agents erupted into laughter.[5]

This passage comes at the beginning of a chapter about how and why video dealers took on great personal risk at a time when the government of Iran had made possessing and distributing videocassettes a criminal offense. The vivid story of Hamid's encounter with immigration officials helps to support Atwood's argument about the cultural significance of video during a time of government oppression. The concrete details don't delay the reader from getting to the point. On the contrary, they draw the reader into the high-stakes network of underground video dealers that will be the main subject of the chapter. When selecting descriptive details to share in your own writing, prioritize those that are most relevant to the broader points you'll be making. Including descriptive detail for its own sake can lead to overly flowery prose that will try the patience of academic readers who are ultimately reading instrumentally.

Another way to enliven your text is to incorporate personal details that invite a sense of human connection between yourself and your reader. You might decide to disclose your own motivations for conducting your research or weave yourself and your experiences into the narrative of your manuscript. Another example comes from the introduction to Lilly Irani's book *Chasing Innovation: Making Entrepreneurial Citizens in Modern India*:

> I wrote this ethnography not just for my scholarly fields or the "general public"—whoever that is. I wrote it for friends at DevDesign and beyond as they sensed the inadequacies of innovation practices in ways that manifested as cynicism, jadedness, or burnout. I wrote for those who see hope in the labor of making technologies in the struggle for a better life, but who might find wisdom and forewarning in the frustrations of the entrepreneurial citizens who people this book. . . . Those I worked with in Delhi called on me to recognize the similarities between my biography and theirs. "You're just like us," a graphic designer and friend of studio members told me six months into fieldwork. I do not take this statement for granted but rather as a puzzle.[6]

In this passage, the details Irani shares and the tone in which she shares them reveals, rather than conceals, her attachment to her research and shows that she is not merely writing about abstractions. By making similar moves, you too can offer your reader a reason to be attached to your work.

Assessment questions:

> Is your tone consistent throughout the text?
> Is your tone appropriate for your intended readership?
> Do you use vivid description and personal perspective
>   appropriately to forge a connection with your readers?

Clear Up Sentence-Level Obfuscations

Your manuscript may have issues with grammar, mechanics, and other technical matters that fall under the purview of copyediting and therefore don't need to be addressed at this stage. Make note of these issues in a general way at this point—so you can remember to address them later—but don't try to identify, let alone correct them, right now. Focusing on such issues before manuscript development is complete is counterproductive, because doing so may dampen your confidence in your writing skills or distract you from more urgent developmental concerns. However, you may want to watch out for a few stylistic issues that arise at the sentence level, because they can obscure substantive aspects of your argument and impede your connection with your reader.

The first of these sentence-level issues is overuse of specialist language, or jargon, which I've defined as "language that your reader will only understand if they've read the same stuff you've read."[7] It can be hard to identify jargon in your own writing, and if you're writing for other experts in your field who likely have read the same material as you, extensive use of jargon may not be a problem. However, if you're writing for interdisciplinary readers, students, or readers outside the academy, such readers may not have previously encountered all your specialist terms. Search critically for such terms in your manuscript and make a note to either come up with a plain-language substitute or integrate a concise definition of the term into the flow of your text so that you're teaching your nonspecialist readers as you go.[8]

A second stylistic issue that arises at the sentence level is the use of passive voice in ways that conceal actors, power relationships, and the direction of cause and effect. For example, your manuscript might contain a statement like "Banned movie content was available in Iran through an expansive dissemination infrastructure." In this (made up) sentence, we learn that a dissemination infrastructure existed that made banned videos available, but we don't learn who built the infrastructure, let alone why it was built or with what consequences. Such omissions obfuscate power relationships, which is the opposite of what many academic writers want to do. The statement could be constructed more actively as, "It was not just that Iranians gained access to banned movie content but also that people developed and sustained an expansive infrastructure that disseminated video."[9] Here (in the published sentence), we readers understand more clearly that Iranians actively resisted the government's ban on videocassettes by building their own illicit distribution infrastructure. Passive phrasing, like the other stylistic issues I mention in this section, is not in and of itself incorrect. It may work well in your text, depending on the information provided in the other sentences around it. Attune yourself to noticing passive constructions and decide in context whether they undermine the force of your argument and thus the meaning and impact of your work overall.

You may notice that your writing slips into passive voice when you are making strong claims that you privately feel hesitant about committing to. Relatedly, you may use tentative or what I call "hedgy" language to soften your arguments for fear of objection by some imagined reader.[10] For instance, your thesis statement could look something like this: "It is possible that conflicts over lifestyle practices could detract from feelings of solidarity among radical activists, which may weaken their efforts at collective political organizing." Contingent language like this can be acceptable—I use it throughout this book and in this very sentence—because contingency and nuance are often called for in scholarly work. Indeed, you'll want to avoid overreaching with your claims, and, "as paradoxical as it seems, you [will] make your argument stronger and more credible by modestly acknowledging its limits."[11] However, as an editor, I encourage authors to trim hedgy language when possible, because if your manuscript doesn't appear to advance research-supported claims that you can strongly stand behind, it may elicit little interest from publishers or readers. The preceding example sentence could easily be restated as, "My research shows that conflicts over lifestyle practices detract from feelings of solidarity among radical activists, impeding their efforts at collective political organizing." If you don't feel you can stand behind the version of your argument with hedgy language removed, revisit your research to figure out which claims you are prepared to support with the evidence you've gathered and the analysis you've performed.

Overly long sentences are another stylistic issue that warrants addressing during the developmental stage, especially if such sentences tend to crop up when you're trying to express complex ideas. Ambiguous use of pronouns—overusing "this," "that," "it," and so on, without tying them to clear referents—can also cloud your text's intended meaning. When you're stating a key aspect of your argument or contribution, be sure your reader doesn't miss the point because it's buried in a complicated sentence structure or made unclear by an ambiguous pronoun. The use of pronouns and long, complex sentences aren't problematic in themselves; they only become troublesome when they interfere with your reader absorbing other fundamental aspects of your manuscript.

Pay particular attention to these sentence-level issues at the key points in your text where the publishability of your ideas may be decided. In other words, look closely at the places where you articulate your main argument and contribution. If you followed my procedure for marking up your draft, you can focus on the underlined passages. Also look closely at the first pages of your manuscript and of each chapter, because your preliminary readers will form their first impressions of your writing there. The issues I described may also appear in other parts of your text, but you can likely address them in the last stages of manuscript preparation before your text goes into production. Even if peer reviewers note such issues, they're unlikely to make or break a publisher's decision to acquire your book.

Again, many stylistic problems can and should be handled at a later phase of the publishing process, after the fundamentals of the text are in place (Chapter 10). Understanding where you are in the manuscript development and publication process is key. Knowing that a finer level of editing will happen later can free you up to concentrate on the major issues first when it comes to the style of your manuscript.

Assessment questions:

Are your key points unencumbered by sentence-level
issues such as:
Specialist terminology?
Passive constructions?
Hedgy language?
Long or overly complex sentences?
Ambiguous pronouns?

A Few Words of Encouragement

WHAT EMOTIONS might you be feeling at this point in the manuscript development cycle? The process of assessing a manuscript for development opportunities can feel empowering, because you finally have a systematic way to revise your draft. However, the process can also raise negative emotions such as shame about the problems you perceive in your manuscript, overwhelm at the work ahead, fear you won't develop your manuscript effectively, or resistance to a new approach to your writing and editing practices. Do you doubt whether your manuscript can even be salvaged? Do you contemplate giving up on the whole business of trying to publish it? If you're feeling any of these things, know that such responses are normal.

Even as a developmental editor who works on manuscripts for other writers, I usually experience a several-days-long stretch in each job where I feel a pit in my stomach about the critiques I'm going to have to share with the author about their manuscript. Even though the author sought me out because they knew they needed help, they might have been privately hoping I'd make a few quick suggestions and say the rest looks great. I empathize with the anxiety an author may feel when they learn that their manuscript needs a lot of work. Fortunately, the pit in my stomach tends to go away as I continue with my process and move past the assessment phase. Once I start writing up an editorial plan, I feel more certain about the author's ability to carry out the necessary changes and arrive at a much-improved manuscript. I also remind myself that the text belongs to the author, and they get to make their own editorial decisions about it. My role is to offer support that they might not otherwise get, just as the role of this book is to offer you tools you may not find elsewhere.

Trust the process for now. Allow yourself to feel the negative emotions—which are valid. You will feel better when you get to the next phase, in which you'll make your editorial plan and execute your edits. The next part of this book is all about the power of the editorial plan and how it puts you back in control over your manuscript. As painful as the assessment phase may be, its upside is that it gives you data with which to make informed decisions about where you'll spend your time and effort. As you move forward, recognize that you can still publish an outstanding book without pursuing every possible opportunity to develop your manuscript.

In the meantime, give yourself credit where it's due. At least a few of the assessment questions in the previous chapters likely revealed things your text is already doing well. Put a big smiley face by those items or cross them out on your checklist (see Appendix A) as a way of acknowledging your accomplishments thus far.

If you've discovered many development opportunities in your manuscript, you're in excellent company. Everything in the previous chapters has come from my work with hundreds of scholarly authors like yourself. Many of those authors went on to land book contracts, publish their books, and receive positive reviews and even awards. No manuscript starts out perfect, and all manuscripts take multiple rounds of revision to get to their publishable form. The fact that you care enough about your work to read this book and get to this point indicates that you're capable of continuing with the development process and producing a stellar text.

PHASE III

Plan and Execute Your Edits

IF PHASE II of the manuscript development cycle is complete, you can now formulate an editorial plan to help you revise your manuscript in a systematic way. Moving from assessment to planning marks a clear and embodied shift from a reactive mode in which you might be thinking, "Oh no, look at all these problems in my text," to an executive mode in which you can say, "I'm in charge of this text and I get to decide what I'm going to do with it." You're now not just the author of your text but also its editor.

The questionnaire you filled out in Phase I is a tool to assist you in making suitable choices for your manuscript. In that questionnaire, you named the readers you want to reach and prioritized your potential audiences based on your broader goals. You can now evaluate which development opportunities are most urgent to pursue to make a strong connection with your highest-priority readers.

Planning involves both synthesizing and filtering, because you may lack the time or capacity to do everything your manuscript might invite you to do. If you treat the developmental opportunities you found during your assessment as invitations, then planning allows you to choose which invitations to accept. To some opportunities, you might say, "Thank you for the invitation, but I'd rather not," or "Let's check in later and see if that will work in my schedule." Go back to the questions you answered in Phase I about external timeline constraints and competing demands on your mental, physical, and emotional labor. With these practical factors in mind, make the editorial choices that are reasonable for your actual circumstances, not the choices you might make in a nonexistent perfect world.

In the next two chapters, you'll learn how to write an editorial plan for your text, much as a professional developmental editor would do for a client's manuscript. The editorial plan is composed of two parts: a high-level editorial summary (Chapter 8) and an itemized set of edits that you will execute (Chapter 9). You'll write up both parts of your plan before going back into your manuscript and making any changes. Chapter 10 will offer tips on altering your text once your plan is in place.

Why take the time to write up a plan first, when you could be spending that time getting your edits done? A plan allows you to see at a glance everything that needs to be done, which helps you to decide the order you want to do it in and the time you want to devote to each task. Your editorial plan can also be shared with your publisher, especially if you've been asked to write a response memo describing the revisions you'll be making in light of peer reviewer reports (Chapter 1). You may be able to use your editorial plan in proposals for course releases or funding support; your plan will demonstrate that you'll make good use of any time and resources you may be granted to help you finish your book. Furthermore, your plan will serve as a concrete blueprint for the work ahead. Even if you end up needing to take a long break from working on your manuscript, your plan will enable you to pick up right where you left off in the manuscript development cycle.

The best reason to make a plan before beginning your edits is that it puts you in control over your manuscript. Just as the process of writing your manuscript allows you to figure out and organize what you think about your subject matter, the process of writing your editorial plan allows you to figure out and organize your thoughts about your book. You will no longer be driven by your immediate reactions to the text as its writer or reader. Now you get to be the developmental editor.

8

Draft Your Editorial Summary

LIKE MANY academics, your previous experiences with having your work "edited" may have involved handing a draft to a professor or advisor for feedback. Sometime later, you received the draft back, marked up with comments and possibly several strikethroughs and suggested additions. You then attempted to address all the comments and suggestions one by one, hopefully arriving at an improved draft. This sequence is typical of editing in college and graduate school, and it might even be adequate for polishing shorter pieces of writing, but professional developmental editors don't approach a manuscript this way.

As an editor, I might return an annotated draft to an author with suggested edits, but I also want to help the author get deeper insight into their text. I want them to understand both what changes to make and why the changes will lead to a text that's more effectively aligned with the author's goals and readerships. And I want to support my author in executing the needed edits by giving an overview of all the work ahead before pointing them to individual revisions. For these reasons, my key deliverable as a developmental editor is a letter that summarizes both my assessment and my recommended edits at a high level.

Because you're now the developmental editor of your manuscript, I encourage you to adopt the practice of writing editorial summaries for yourself. To write your editorial summary, you'll filter your impressions of the manuscript that you recorded during the assessment phase and synthesize the most consequential ones into a holistic revision plan. Having assessed all the development opportunities you *could* pursue, your summary will document the opportunities you *will* pursue, describing both the problems you identified and the solutions you'll implement to fix them. Because you're dealing with fundamental issues that may affect your entire text, you'll describe those issues at a high level and propose comprehensive remedies that may include substantive reconceptualization and reorganization of the manuscript. Scribbling notes in the margins of your draft isn't enough to communicate those kinds of revisions.

Your editorial summary needn't be formatted like an actual letter, or even in complete paragraphs and sentences. You might instead craft your summary as a list of bullet points that you handwrite in a notebook or array in a spreadsheet. Your summary might be jotted down on a series of sticky notes or notecards that you can engage with in a tactile way and reorganize as needed. You might draw a visual map. Any format that helps you organize your editorial thoughts and understand your revision plan is fine. Just keep your editorial summary separate from your manuscript, so you can work on the summary and later consult it without getting distracted by the content of the text itself.

You can also use your summary to put needed distance between yourself as the author who wrote your manuscript and your new role as the editor who is going to change it. One of the preliminary readers for this book found herself writing an editorial letter to herself in second person, addressing herself as "you" as if she were a professional editor sharing a summary with a client. Another preliminary reader depersonalized the editing process even further, writing a letter that addressed "the manuscript" without addressing the writer at all. This is a situation in which passive voice is acceptable if it helps you do the necessary work.

The Content of Your Editorial Summary

In this section, I offer you a template for your editorial summary that includes nine essential parts. The summary template is structured as a linearly written document—much like the letters I write for my authors—but you can adapt the template as needed if you're using a different format for your summary. The level of detail you include in your summary is also up to you. As you become more familiar with the manuscript development process, you'll learn whether you find more or less detailed summaries helpful when it comes time to execute your edits (see Appendix B for a sample editorial summary).

Here's an overview of the nine essential parts of your editorial summary:

1. Major parameters of the text
2. Goals and intended readerships for the text
3. Any previous feedback that your edits should address
4. High-level summary of planned edits to develop the text's argument
5. High-level summary of planned edits to develop the text's evidence
6. High-level summary of planned edits to develop the text's structure
7. High-level summary of planned edits to develop the text's style

8. Mini summaries of smaller units within the text, as needed

9. Next steps, in order of priority

Begin your editorial summary with a synopsis of the major parameters of the project: the topic, scope, approach, and your overall purpose in writing it. You can copy and paste these parameters from your questionnaire answers in Phase I. The synopsis will be particularly helpful if you have to put your manuscript aside for a while and return to it later, or if you want to share your editorial summary with someone else, such as your publisher, who may need a reminder of what your book is about.

Second, recap your goals and intended readerships, focusing on those that are highest priority for you. Again, you can pull these from your Phase I questionnaire. If you skipped the questionnaire before, take the time to clarify your goals and readerships now. The key here is to establish why you are making changes to develop your manuscript. Edits that don't get you closer to your goals or your most desired readers may be unworthy of the effort.

Third, write down any key feedback you've received about your manuscript that needs to be taken into account. Even if you summarized this feedback in your Phase I questionnaire, refer back to your peer review reports and any correspondence with your publisher, if applicable. Our memories of feedback are easily distorted, in both positive and negative directions. Reacquaint yourself with what reviewers said so you can respond appropriately. You may want to copy down the most relevant feedback into your summary verbatim so that you have an accurate picture as you move forward.

Now begin outlining the developmental opportunities you identified during your assessment. I recommend organizing this part of the summary in four parts, one for each of the four pillars: argument, evidence, structure, and style.

I always address argument first in my editorial summaries, because a scholarly text's argument is often its reason to exist (Chapter 4). In my experience, any adjustments made to the text's core argument will affect everything else, so they should be settled first. In your summary, state the main argument as currently articulated in the text and note where it's articulated. If no main argument is articulated in the text, state the tacit argument that drives the book. If your book has other points that need to be argued to support the main argument, write those out too.

If your assessment has shown that your argument needs to change in some way, here's where you can describe how and why. Are there too many arguments competing for prominence? Does your main argument need to shift in order to work as a driving thesis for the entire book? Should your argument be adjusted to answer a "why" or "how" question in addition to a "what" question? Do you need to more precisely define the concepts your argument rests on? Could the stakes of your argument feel inconsequential to the readers you're trying to reach? If necessary, put forth a few candidates for better arguments here in your summary.

After summarizing how you plan to develop your text's argument, turn to evidence. As you did with argument, give a general summary of how evidence and analysis are currently functioning in the manuscript as detected during your assessment. Then describe any changes you're planning. Does any evidence need to be added, more effectively analyzed, or relocated to better support the text's arguments? Will you be removing any irrelevant or redundant evidence? Stick to the big picture; don't describe every piece of evidence that you'll be touching with your edits.

Instead summarize the general flavor of how you plan to develop the use of evidence in your manuscript.

Next, summarize your text's structural needs. Structure is commonly the most extensive area for development, so you may write quite a bit in this portion of your editorial summary. Your discussion of structure may benefit from being subdivided into matters of organization, signaling, and length.

If your book needs major reorganization at the chapter level, explain why and then write out a new table of contents that illustrates how you plan to develop the structure. If material needs to be moved across chapters, explain that here as well. Including outlines in your editorial summary can be helpful, because they serve as blueprints to follow when you start moving things around. When developing an entire book, a major reorganization can quickly become unwieldy and confusing, especially if you can't accomplish all the moves in one sitting. The outline in your summary will become your point of reference to keep you aligned with an overall editorial vision, even when you're at risk of losing sight of the forest while transplanting individual trees.

If you plan to restructure individual chapters or sections within chapters—without moving material across chapters—summarize those lower-level structural edits in a separate section of your editorial summary to be dealt with later.

After describing any plans for reorganization, summarize other structural issues you found during your assessment such as titles, headings, topic sentences, breaks, and transitions that should be further developed. Don't try to document every instance where an edit is needed or come up with the perfect chapter titles or transitions right now. Choose a few prime examples that illustrate the issues you've observed, then summarize the general kinds of changes you intend to make and why.

If you noticed length issues during your assessment, lay out your plan for reducing or increasing length or for bringing the lengths of component parts into balance. Write down how much needs to be trimmed or added and give a general summary of the material you'll be cutting, inserting, or relocating. Alternatively, you can articulate your justification for not making changes if you've decided to go against convention in this area.

After discussing argument, evidence, and structure, summarize any stylistic matters that need attention. Again, record a general sense of the stylistic issues you've identified and the editorial solutions you're planning to execute. Include a representative example or two from the text, if you find them helpful to illustrate why stylistic development is required.

Once you've summarized the issues that affect your manuscript as a whole, you may want to address smaller units within the text that will need developmental attention. For example, if one specific chapter of your book needs a clearer sub-argument or would benefit from internal restructuring, you can now write a mini editorial summary for that chapter in particular. Your miniature summary can establish the parameters of the individual chapter in terms of topic, scope, approach, and purpose of the chapter in the larger manuscript; then address argument, evidence, structure, and style issues in that chapter as needed.

Throughout the parts of your editorial summary, be sure to praise your text wherever praise is due. For instance, you might note that the structure of Chapter 4 is particularly effective, or you might point out that Chapter 2 makes great use of analysis to connect its evidence with its arguments. Acknowledging your manuscript's strengths carries a dual function. First, it keeps your morale up, because listing nothing but problems can easily make you feel discouraged about your skill as a writer.

Second, praise can help you recognize where certain parts of your manuscript can serve as models or templates to emulate in other parts.

I also encourage you to spell out the "why" behind any problems you identify and any editorial solutions you propose in your summary. Why is this particular aspect of the manuscript causing it not to work as a whole? Why will your planned revisions help your manuscript do the work you want it to do? Include these justifications, first, to remind yourself of the purpose and payoff of your manuscript development work. Second, pushing yourself to justify each area for development can help you prioritize which work is most essential and, in some cases, illuminate that some development opportunities aren't worth pursuing after all. As a professional editor, I wouldn't expect my authors to accept every edit I suggested unless I could give them a good reason why they should. If you find that a justification boils down to, "this is how a professor told me to do it when I was a grad student," but you don't see how doing it that way would help you connect more effectively with your readers, maybe the edit isn't necessary to include in your plan.

In documenting your reasons for pursuing certain development opportunities, you may also find that some reasons are more urgent than others, which can help you prioritize which edits to execute at which stage. For example, a change for which your reason is "to help my preliminary readers better appreciate my argument and contribution" will be crucial to attend to if you're at the pre-submission stage of manuscript development. In contrast, a stylistic change for which your reason is "to keep my tone consistent across the text" might be saved for the final round of manuscript development before publication. This discussion of how to order and prioritize your edits leads to the final component of the editorial summary: next steps.

Close Your Summary by Listing Next Steps in Order of Priority

At the end of your editorial summary, lay the groundwork for actually executing your planned edits by explicitly outlining your next steps. You may decide that some development opportunities should be pursued before submitting your manuscript to preliminary readers, whereas other opportunities can be considered at a later stage, after you've received external feedback. Remember that you'll likely repeat the manuscript development cycle multiple times throughout your publishing process, so some issues can be put on hold and dealt with later. You can still include the less urgent issues in your editorial summary, but note what doesn't need to be addressed immediately.

The order of your next steps will also take into account edits that can't be executed until other changes are complete. For example, you won't be able to address the structural signaling in your manuscript until the organization is in place. And some changes may obviate others. For instance, if several pieces of evidence need more analysis to connect them to an argument, it would make sense to deal with those after you've solidified what you want your book's argument to be. Some of that evidence might get cut from the manuscript altogether because it isn't strictly relevant to the argument you land on. In such a case it wouldn't be a good use of your time to generate more analysis before refining the argument. You may be unable to anticipate which editorial changes will impact others or how. You may even plan to conduct additional mini assessments after certain edits are made to see what issues may have been taken care of or newly introduced. But to the best of your ability, try to devise a logical sequence of edits so you are expending your effort when and where it will be most productive.

Your time and resources for developing your manuscript are finite (Chapter 2). In fact, you may realize while drafting your editorial summary that you won't have enough time or capacity to develop your manuscript in all the ways you might like to. Such a realization calls for you to ponder what editor Maron L. Waxman calls a "hierarchy of changes," in which you categorize each type of edit you plan to make as "necessary, felicitous, [or] meticulous."[1] With such categories in place, you can start with the necessary edits before proceeding to the felicitous and meticulous ones as circumstances allow.

After drawing up your summary, you may discover that even the most necessary changes—those that could make or break your book's acceptance for publication and its reception by your most important readers—won't be executable in the time you have available. If you find yourself in this scenario, return to your Phase I questionnaire and identify where there might be flexibility to negotiate more time or resources. You may need to ask for an extension from your publisher, or you may need to more aggressively defend your manuscript development work from competing demands on your time.

You can also reevaluate your goals in light of your constraints. For example, perhaps you're writing your first book, aiming to earn tenure in your home department of political science. You also want your book to be adopted in interdisciplinary gender studies courses, so your editorial plan includes incorporating additional evidence and analysis that bolsters your project's feminist framework. Furthermore, you'd like your book to be useful to feminist activists outside the academy, so you want to overhaul the writing style to be more appealing to nonacademic readers. When you look at all these elements of your plan, you may realize they simply aren't possible to execute in the time you have available. Reevaluating your goals might mean refocusing on your core contribution to the field of political science so that your book remains a strong element of your tenure case. You might decide that your next book could incorporate a more prominent gender component and that you could publish a zine and do a few podcast interviews to reach the activist audience after the tenure book is finished. In short, you may have to let go of some of your hopes for this particular book. These can be difficult, painful decisions to make, but with an editorial plan in place, at least you'll have clarity about when and why the decisions must be made. You can always save some goals for future projects.

After drafting your editorial summary, you'll move on to the second part of your editorial plan, which is an itemized to-do list of each specific change you'll make to your text. Your summary was a high-level overview of the work ahead; your itemized to-do list will take your editorial plan down to the keystroke, showing exactly how you'll execute your developmental edits.

Chapter 9 will cover how to make your itemized list of edits, but what about order of operations? I strongly recommend writing the editorial summary before itemizing your edits. Some users of this book will want to skip the summary and jump to planning the individual edits. For many writers, that will be the path of least resistance because it will be closer to how you're accustomed to editing your own work. However, effective developmental editing requires that your plan remains aligned with the big picture. Each individual edit should have a justification behind it related to ensuring that your text's argument, evidence, structure, and style serve your goals and intended readers. Your summary is where you articulate those justifications, so please don't skip it.

You might be tempted to itemize your individual edits first and then reverse engineer an editorial summary by grouping the edits together and generalizing about them at a higher level. If that feels more comfortable to you than writing the summary first, go ahead and do that for now. But be sure to write up the summary before executing your edits. By training your summarization muscles, you'll soon gain the skill to sketch your editorial summary before enumerating specific edits, which will ultimately make your developmental editing process more efficient and effective in the long run.

9

Itemize Your Edits

HAVING DRAFTED your high-level editorial summary, you can now turn to the second component of your editorial plan, which is an itemized set of all the developmental edits you will execute. Although it might feel like an arduous extra step to write out all your edits before implementing them, itemizing your edits in advance carries several benefits. First, itemizing your edits will help you get a handle on the total amount of work you must do and make it easier to tackle that work in short sessions if that's all you have available. Second, if your editorial plan is full of large, intimidating tasks like "restructure Chapter 4," your itemized list will break that down into manageable pieces such as, "move three paragraphs on X up to the section about Y," "group all discussions of Z in a new section at the end of the chapter," and "insert a section break and new heading between the discussions of A and B." Third, specific editorial instructions can reduce decision fatigue and allow you to jump right into editing whenever you find the time for it. Finally, the best order to execute your edits may vary from the order in which the problems appear in the text. By indicating all the edits before actually making them, you'll be better equipped to decide which edits to complete first.

Your itemized list of edits doesn't have to be formatted as an actual list. You can instead embed a series of editorial notes in your manuscript to indicate the specific locations where changes will be made. These notes are distinct from any notes you might have made on your text during the assessment phase (Chapter 3), which expressed your immediate reactions to the text as you read it. Therefore, you'll want to embed your new, curated editorial notes in a clean version of your document, free from the visual chaos of your previous assessment notes. (For an example of how editorial notes might be embedded into a real manuscript, see Appendix B.)

You can also make an actual list of editing to-dos if that appeals to you. Some writers prefer a separate list, stored in a new text file or spreadsheet, because it keeps the manuscript document itself uncluttered. A list also allows you to cross off your completed items as you go, which brings a satisfying sense of accomplishment to a sometimes tedious process.

How to Itemize Your Edits

Developmental editors prescribe five essential types of changes when editing a manuscript: inserting new material, rewriting or reframing specific passages, cutting or condensing specific passages, moving blocks of text around, and inserting or closing up breaks in the text (Figure 9.1).

These types of edits may encompass changes within any of the four pillars of argument, evidence, structure, and style. And any of them may be used in service of any of the various opportunities for development discussed in Chapters 4 through 7. Breaking your planned edits down into these types will bring order to the revision process for you. It's less daunting to deal with complex issues in your text when you see that there are

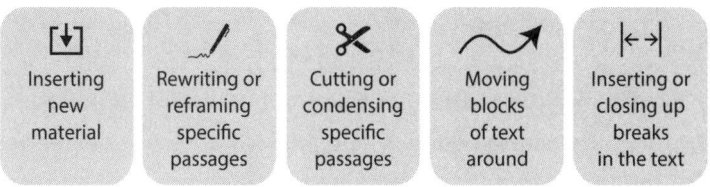

FIGURE 9.1. Five essential changes made during
manuscript development

only a handful of kinds of tasks to undertake. So, how can you
indicate each type of edit in your manuscript to facilitate execu-
tion of your editorial plan?

Inserting new material. Your developmental assessment
may have identified additional material that would enhance
your manuscript. Table 9.1 presents examples of such additional
material. Not all of the examples in the table will apply to your
text. You may want to cross out those that don't appear in your
editorial summary or circle those that do.

TABLE 9-1. Insertions to be made during manuscript development

Argument	Clear statement of the book's main argument Articulation of the text's scholarly contribution Precise definitions of key concepts
Evidence	Additional evidence to support particular arguments More extensive analysis of the evidence offered More discussion of the connection between evidence and arguments
Structure	New titles and headings Topic sentences at the beginnings of paragraphs and sections Transitional language between different ideas
Style	More vivid description of research objects or settings

Embed a comment or insert a placeholder in the flow of your text to indicate where each insertion should occur. When putting placeholders in the text, it can be helpful to include a unique character sequence (e.g., ##) or a rarely used set of braces (e.g., {}), so that these insertions are easy to find and remove later, after the additional material has been inserted. Your embedded placeholder could look something like this: ##Insert new heading here.##

You can facilitate your editing process even more effectively by spelling out both the nature of the additional material and its purpose in your comment or placeholder as concretely as you can at this point. Note any ideas you may have about the precise length of the required additions as a reminder of how much work is necessary so you don't try to do more. For example, your comment might say something like, ##Add a brief paragraph here to explain why this story of X is important in a broader sense. What does the case of X illuminate about Y in general?## or ##Consider adding one more sentence here to drive home the contribution of this research##.

Rewriting or reframing specific passages. In some instances you won't insert substantial new material but rather alter sections of text that already exist in the manuscript. Table 9.2 presents example edits of this type. When marking these passages in your text, embed a comment at the beginning of the passage explaining how and why the text needs to be rewritten or reframed. Then highlight or mark the text so that the end of the passage in question is clear.

Cutting or condensing specific passages. Your assessment may also have alerted you to material that should be removed or shortened in length. Common examples of material that could be candidates for such trimming are:

TABLE 9-2. Edits that involve rewriting or reframing

Argument	Changing wording so that you're using terms consistently across the text and emphasizing key concepts where they occur Articulating your argument in a new way so that its significance and portability are clear
Evidence	Changing how you present primary source evidence so that your own words and interpretation are more prominent
Structure	Improving titles and headings so that they convey both the topic and your take on the topic Refining transitional language to expose the precise relationship between ideas
Style	Adjusting how you present quoted material Tempering tone to hit the right emotional register, level of formality, etc. Substituting plain language for obscure jargon or incorporating definitions of specialist terms Turning passive constructions to active where necessary Strengthening hedgy language Recrafting sentences to clarify core ideas

- Tangential arguments that don't support the text's main thesis, along with any evidence or analysis in support of those arguments
- Extraneous data or examples to illustrate arguments that are already sufficiently supported in the text
- Long blocks of primary source material, if you don't have any interpretation or analysis to add
- Unnecessary images that don't enhance the reader's understanding of your arguments
- Excessive discussion of methods and methodology
- Evidence from another scholar's research
- Excessive notes

You can mark these passages much as you do those to be rewritten or reframed.

Moving blocks of text around. The blocks of text that you move around during developmental editing might be whole chapters, sections within chapters, paragraphs, or even sentences or phrases. When considering sentences and phrases, remember that the point of manuscript development isn't to polish the prose. Polishing comes later, with line editing. Only manipulate small chunks of text at this point if doing so will affect how a fundamental aspect of the manuscript, such as its argument, will connect with readers. Edits that involve rearranging existing text include:

- Moving contextual explanations closer to the key points they support
- Grouping discussions of a single topic together
- Moving material to ensure that discrete sections are focused and cohesive around their arguments
- Moving material into or out of specific textual units to adhere to genre conventions, e.g., moving evidence and analysis from an introduction chapter into a body chapter
- Moving elegant summations of your text's topic and your take on the topic into titles, headings, and topic sentences

As you annotate these edits, highlight text that needs to be moved and embed a comment near the highlighted text to indicate the rough location it should be moved to. Page numbers are immaterial in such notes, because the pagination will change as you execute other edits. I prefer to indicate the new location in relation to other parts of the text, for example, "move this sentence to immediately after the paragraph about X," or to insert a placeholder in the flow of the text where I think the material should go, for example, "bring the four paragraphs about Y from Chapter 4 to this spot." Also note any additional edits necessitated by the move, such as the need for new transitional language around the transplanted passage.[1]

Inserting or closing up breaks in the text. When noting breaks to be inserted or closed up, you may be considering breaks between chapters, sections, or paragraphs. You may need to insert a break within a single sentence, if a key idea is getting lost. Remember that breaks in the text tell readers that one complete idea or line of argument has been wrapped up and a new one is being broached. Executing this type of edit may be as simple as one or two keystrokes, yet I still recommend itemizing these edits in advance and doing the implementation later. It's easy to get caught up in fiddling with the exact location of the break and in massaging the surrounding text to make the break feel organic. For now, note the approximate location of the break with a placeholder or embedded comment and explain why it's needed or not needed. (To see various types of edits itemized on a few pages of sample text, consult Appendix B.)

Keeping Edits in Scope with Your Plan

It's important that your editorial summary and your itemized edits remain in tight correspondence with each other. Keep your summary close by when embedding notes in your text to avoid the temptation to indicate edits that fall outside the scope of your plan, such as line edits or copyedits. All edits at this stage should be made expressly in service of the four pillars of your text—argument, evidence, structure, and style. That means you will be undertaking developmental edits to better express your argument, better support your argument with evidence and analysis, better communicate your argument via the structure of the text, and better reflect your own voice and approach to the subject matter.

This isn't to say that you must flout all sentence-level edits during the manuscript development process. If a sentence-level change—a change to the structure of a sentence, a different wording, a clarification of pronouns or terminology—would allow you to more effectively communicate your argument, your evidence, the structure of the text, or your authorial voice, then such changes may be appropriate right now. However, if you find that these types of small edits are occurring every few sentences, step back and look for bigger issues at the root of the frequent stylistic adjustments. For instance, if hedgy language and passive constructions appear consistently throughout your manuscript, you may need to refine your argument so you can more confidently stand behind it. Once that global work is done—which may entail substantive reframing of the manuscript—the stylistic issues may solve themselves as you do your rewriting.

At this stage, don't worry about whether your manuscript's prose is aesthetically appealing or follows technical grammatical conventions. Don't pay attention to formatting or other physical aspects of the text, other than making sure headings and subheadings are organized logically. You will eventually deal with lower-level matters after the current manuscript development cycle has run its course.

If you're already under contract with a publisher, I recommend running your plan by your acquiring editor before executing edits, especially if you intend to make substantial changes. If your manuscript has yet to be approved for publication by the press's editorial board, you'll likely be asked to write a formal response to the peer reviews (Chapter 1). Your editorial plan can serve as the basis for that response. When you share the plan with your publisher, also discuss a realistic date for returning your edited manuscript. Your editorial summary plus itemized edits will help your acquiring editor see precisely what work you need to do, and it may justify a longer timeline than originally anticipated.

If you want to seek feedback from other parties before executing your edits, you can do that as well. Alternatively, you may decide to wait to seek outside support until after you've completed your developmental edits and have a new version of the manuscript to share. (Appendix C covers how to seek that support whether before or after your edits are complete.)

You may reach a point, either before or during editing, where you believe that finishing your book would require more work than it's worth. In some cases, that belief might be rational. If so, the time you've spent on assessment and planning will still have been productive because you'll have a greater sense of certainty about your decision to move on. You won't have to look back and think, "What if I had just tried a little bit to fix that manuscript?" The manuscript development cycle will have shown you precisely how much work it would have taken.

If you find yourself fantasizing about quitting at this point, look back at Chapters 1 and 2 and at the words of encouragement following Chapter 7. Reconnecting with your goals and with your current circumstances will clarify your decision either way. Everyone has difficult writing and editing days. Of the hundreds of intelligent and hard-working academic authors I've worked with, not a single one has found it easy to publish a book. Don't give up on your book unless doing so is truly aligned with your goals.

10

Alter Your Text

CONGRATULATIONS! YOU'VE nearly completed an entire
round of the manuscript development cycle: You clarified
your mission for your manuscript; you assessed it for opportunities to develop its argument, evidence, structure, and
style; and you made an editorial plan. Once you've cleared
your editorial plan with your publisher and received feedback
from any other readers if applicable, you'll be all set to execute
the edits in your plan. In this chapter, I'll share five broad
pieces of advice to guide you as you alter your text. I'll then
describe the levels of editing that follow developmental editing and leave you with a preview of your role in the editorial
processes that will occur after you submit your final manuscript for publication.

Five Tips for Executing Your Edits

Keep your editorial plan handy and use it as a blueprint.
Don't squander the work you've done by straying away from
the plan or second-guessing your assessment. At the same time,
be flexible. You can amend your plan and reorder your priorities
if necessary. Write amendments into the plan as they come

up—using different color text, if you like—so the plan stays current and you have a record of your decision-making.

Save your work frequently. Double-check that you have a saved version of your manuscript before you start making changes so that you'll know which version you did your assessment on. As I execute edits, I make a new version of my manuscript file with a new file name every day, putting the date right into the file name.

When removing material from your draft, copy it into an overflow document that you can dip back into if necessary. You can put whole chapters, sections, paragraphs, sentences, quotations, bibliographic information, or even key words and phrases in this file. Record the date when you removed the material from your draft and the location it came from. This will enable you to find the material easily, if you ever want to put it back in, such as if a peer reviewer wants to see more methodological discussion after you cut most of it out. Be sure to name this document descriptively and store it somewhere readily accessible.

Keep a running list of lower-level edit types that you'll work on after your developmental editing is complete. As you work on your developmental edits, you may spot line editing or copyediting issues that you'll want to address. Resist attending to them while executing your developmental edits. In some work sessions you may not have the capacity for the deep intellectual engagement that developmental editing requires. On such occasions you can work on less demanding editorial tasks, but choose something with a low risk of being obviated by later developmental work. For instance, instead of polishing your prose, assemble your bibliography, focusing on sources you're certain will make it into the final draft.

Allow yourself to stop at some point. In fact, you may have to force yourself to stop, because further development will always be possible. Unless you're preparing the final version of your manuscript before it goes into production, take comfort in the fact that there will be additional opportunities to edit your text before the publishing process is over.

After completing your developmental edits, check your draft against your editorial plan to confirm that you've covered everything. If the text has changed substantially since you last read it all the way through, you might want to do another assessment pass on the new draft. You might also do a quick reassessment on just one part of the manuscript, if you made significant changes to a particular chapter, for instance. You can repeat the steps outlined in Chapter 3 and reapply the diagnostic questions from Chapters 4 through 7 as many times as needed to as many parts of the text as needed, within your time constraints.

After the Developmental Edit

Once your developmental edits are complete—or as complete as you've been able to get them in the current cycle—you can attend to the lower levels of editing before sending the manuscript to its next set of readers. Line editing and copyediting your text can improve the reception of your project by both preliminary and end readers.

Line editing deals with the flow of text and clarity of ideas at the paragraph or sentence level. It involves selecting the words that best express what you mean—diction—and figuring out how to string them together in the most sensical and pleasing way—syntax. Your developmental edit had you remove passages that didn't serve your four pillars, whereas your line edit will have you get rid of repetitive sentences and filler words. You'll look for words and phrases that you overuse, and you'll listen for what editor George Witte calls "the rhythm and movement of lines and sentences."[1] Because you've already handled the major structural issues (Chapter 6), your line edit will be mostly concerned with the style of your text. You've handled some of the stylistic issues already too (Chapter 7), but only where those issues affected major aspects of your text such as your argument and your overall voice. Now you'll do an even more thorough check for style in each line of the manuscript.[2]

Just as line editing could overlap with developmental editing in some instances, so too can it overlap with copyediting, because the boundaries between levels of editing aren't strictly drawn. Whereas line editing ensures that your personal style is coming across consistently and coherently, copyediting is concerned with house style, or a publisher's set of guidelines about the correct presentation of elements in each text. Style in this sense includes rules around grammar, spelling, and punctuation, as well as accurate formatting of references, labeling of figures, and other ancillary aspects of the text.[3] Although every publisher will have their own house style, many scholarly publishers follow well-known style guides such as *The Chicago Manual of Style*.

As the author, you aren't expected to do a professional-level copyedit of your manuscript, meticulously adhering to every rule in the style guide. Your concern should be removing any obvious errors that might confuse your readers, distract them, or cause them to question the carefulness with which you've approached your work. Many scholarly book publishers provide authors with instructions for manuscript preparation, which will tell you which items to focus on. These instructions are often posted on publishers' websites, so you can look up what your intended publisher expects even if you haven't submitted your manuscript for review yet.[4]

In general, your heaviest line editing and copyediting should take place when you're preparing your manuscript for the last time, that is, when you're submitting the final version to your press to be put into production. In my experience, publishers and peer reviewers don't expect perfection in drafts that are under review. Focus on the substance—in terms of argument, evidence, structure, and overall stylistic approach—in the early stages of the publishing process. If you have further developmental work to do, as you likely will at Moment 1 and Moment 2 of the publishing process (Chapter 1), it may be an unfruitful use of your time to meticulously polish your prose and correct every error. Even so, it's vital that your ideas shine through when your project is being evaluated for publication. Some preliminary readers are irrationally persnickety. For this reason, you may want to at least do a quick pass through your manuscript to line edit and copyedit it each time it goes to a new set of readers. Take the care you'd take with any other professional document.

If you're particularly anxious about the judgment you might receive from preliminary readers, consider hiring a professional line editor or copyeditor. However, I would get a second opinion from someone who has experience with the publishing process about whether you truly need professional help. Professional line editing and copyediting can be pricey, so you'll want to make sure the expenditure is necessary before you spend your money, especially when your manuscript is still in the early stages of the publishing process. If you're already in contact with an acquisitions editor who seems supportive of your project, you can ask them whether they think your manuscript requires editing before it goes to peer reviewers. They should have a sense of the level of polish their peer reviewers typically expect.

I've worked with many writers who spoke English as an additional language who worried that their prose could cloud publishers' judgments about their ability to write a book in English. In most cases, their prose was perfectly acceptable and comparable to other writers I've worked with who were able to land book contracts. Publishers do understand that the text will be given a thorough copyedit before publication, so they usually tolerate honest mistakes in the early stages. But again, you may want to get a second opinion about your text just to be sure.

In the final stage, when no developmental editing remains to be done and you're preparing the version of your text that will be published for the world to see, a heavier investment—of time, labor, or money—may be worthwhile. All reputable scholarly publishers will engage a professional copyeditor for your manuscript during the production process, but you may not receive a careful line edit, and the copyedit you get may be largely focused on technical matters, only catching the most glaring grammatical errors. If you want your words and sentences to sing, you'll probably need to put in the effort yourself or hire a professional. (See Appendix C for advice on finding suitable professional editors.)

Your Role in the Production Process

After submitting the final version of your manuscript to your publisher, a production editor or managing editor will oversee the remaining phases of work on your text over the next several months. These phases include professional copyediting followed by proofreading and indexing. As the author you'll be involved in each of these steps to an extent.[5] Ask your editor for a production schedule as soon as possible so you can block out the requisite times on your calendar. You'll likely be given a few weeks or less for each task so it's important to ensure your availability ahead of time.

Your publisher will engage a professional copyeditor to address any errors, inconsistencies, ambiguities, or stylistic quirks that could interfere with reader comprehension and enjoyment. Publishers use house style guides to ensure that the books they publish all basically follow the same conventions for things like punctuation, capitalization, reference formatting, and so on. Each book will have its own style guide as well to make sure that the choices made are self-consistent. If you have certain strong stylistic preferences, such as the use of the singular they, capitalizing the word Black when referring to race, or identity-first language over person-first language—to name a few common examples—make your wishes known to your publisher. In most cases, your publisher and copyeditor will respect your preferences, as long as you're consistent across the text.

If you think of your copyeditor as someone who's there to help by attending to things in your text you haven't been able to attend to, rather than someone who is there to correct you and make you feel bad about all the mistakes you made, you'll find working with a copyeditor to be a positive experience. And you don't have to accept every edit. Copyeditors do sometimes get it wrong when they aren't subject matter specialists and aren't familiar with the idioms and terms of art in your field. I'll never forget how the copyeditor assigned to my first book inexplicably changed all instances of "consumer culture" to "the consumer culture." I'll admit that I got quite irritated while reviewing the edits, but in the end all I had to do was change it back to the correct phrasing, which took about five minutes. You'll likely be given an opportunity to review the copyedits and reject those that aren't in keeping with your authorial intentions. If your copyeditor has fundamentally misunderstood something about your manuscript, causing hours of extra labor for you to correct their mistake, talk to your production editor to see if the problem can be rectified on their end.

Remember that your copyeditor is human. They won't catch every mistake, because no one can achieve 100 percent accuracy in such a technical task. Your publisher may also limit the number of hours your copyeditor is permitted to spend on your manuscript. If you happen to see an error or two after your manuscript has been copyedited—or even after your book is in print—it doesn't mean your copyeditor did a subpar job. To put it in perspective, the copyeditor may have correctly caught hundreds or thousands of errors across your manuscript, so missing a handful is to be expected. This is why it's important for you to go through your text carefully as well, especially at the proofreading stage, because your eyes may catch something that even a thorough copyeditor missed.

Resist interpreting shortness from your copyeditor as criticism or judgment of you as a person or even as a writer. Although the best copyeditors are experts at making their corrections and queries with tact, the highly technical nature of their work may mean that they prioritize directness over diplomacy. The entire existence of copyeditors is predicated on the reality that all texts need help before publication, and most copyeditors are respectful and appreciative of writers, especially those who are respectful and appreciative in return. If you feel that your copyeditor has treated you or your manuscript with hostility or carelessness, bring it up with your production editor to see if they can intervene or offer guidance.[6]

After the text has been copyedited, a designer will lay it out in preparation for printing. Any images will be integrated into the flow of the text, and front and back matter—except for the index—will be put in place. You'll then be sent the typeset page proofs to review for errors, also known as proofreading. Many academic authors handle their own proofreading, but you can hire a professional if you aren't detail-oriented or you don't have time to review the proofs yourself. (Many of the tips in Appendix C on working with a professional developmental editor would also apply to finding a qualified proofreader.)

An index is a map of the ideas in a book and is prepared as one of the final steps before publication. Like copyediting, indexing involves a specialized set of skills and requires formal training to achieve professional standards. Most publishing agreements for scholarly books require the author to furnish their own index, which means you'll have to produce an amateur index yourself or shoulder the cost of hiring a professional to create one. Before you sign a contract with a book publisher, ask if they might provide an indexer and at least charge the cost against your future royalties if not cover the cost outright. In most cases, academic publishers won't be able to accommodate such a request, but the question is reasonable.

If you make your own index, keep in mind that you'll probably be given a minuscule span of time in which to do it, and it'll likely coincide with the period you're given to proofread your text, since indexes must be made from typeset proofs. You can prepare ahead of time by reading up on principles of indexing and by making a preliminary list of all the terms and concepts you would like to appear in your index. You won't be able to map the terms to actual page numbers until you have proofs in hand, but you can save time by knowing what you'll be looking for when the proofs come in. Attempt a high-quality index that your readers will find useful, but don't torment yourself. Make a genuine effort with the tools and time you have, then move on.[7]

If you work with a professional indexer, either one provided by your publisher or funded by yourself, be mindful of two key things. First, you'll want to find an indexer with subject matter expertise or experience indexing books in your field. They'll need to understand your book at a conceptual level to build a usable map for your readers. Second, because of the tight turn-around time given to produce an index, you'll want to start looking for an indexer as soon as you're aware of your book's production schedule. If you start looking for a professional indexer on the day you receive your proofs, you'll be hard-pressed to find someone with the requisite expertise and availability. To find qualified indexers in your field, ask your publisher or colleagues who have had good experiences with their indexers. You can also consult a directory from a professional organization in your home country or region, such as the American Society for Indexing.

Through all these phases—especially from the moment your manuscript is sent to the publisher's professional copyeditor—it's vital to remember that the time for developmental work on the manuscript has passed. Making substantial changes to the text after the professional copyeditor has done their work introduces the risk of new errors. This risk is also why I don't recommend planning to write any major portions of your text, such as your acknowledgments, after professional copyediting has taken place. Once the manuscript is typeset, any significant changes to the text can result in pagination problems or the need to have the manuscript typeset again. Adjustments to the typeset proofs incur costs for your publisher, which they may pass along to you, depending on the terms of your publishing agreement. If you find a major error that needs to be corrected after copyediting and typesetting have taken place—that's what proofreading is for after all—get in touch with your production editor and try to work out a mutually agreeable solution as soon as possible.

Let Your Manuscript Do Its Work

A RUNNING theme in earlier versions of this book manuscript was an idea I called "the good enough draft." My claim was that by applying techniques of developmental editing—by improving a text in the areas of argument, evidence, structure, and style—an author could get their draft to a place where it would be good enough to make a satisfactory impression with readers, even if the text wasn't perfect on every level. A couple of my preliminary readers worried that I might be encouraging academic writers to settle for mediocrity. That wasn't my intention, so I pulled back on this concept of the good enough draft as I revised the manuscript.

But I know my authors. If you've made it to the conclusion of this book, you probably aren't at risk of settling for mediocrity. I don't think you're interested in taking the easy way out. If anything, I suspect you frequently struggle to let your writing go, because you know it could always be better. You expect a lot of yourself; if you didn't, you wouldn't be writing a scholarly book in the first place, let alone reading a whole other book about how to edit it.

So this little conclusion of the book is for my ambitious, conscientious readers, and it's here to encourage you to take the plunge. The prospect of hitting Send on your manuscript can be incredibly nerve-wracking, but your ideas can't reach anyone, let alone do work in the world, if you don't put them out into the world. I hope this book has helped you gain clarity on the work you want your manuscript to be doing and has helped you feel more confident that it will indeed do what you intend it to do. You must eventually let go of the manuscript so it can go do its work.

Doubts are natural. You may worry that a reader you respect will have reasonable objections or that you've missed something important. Perhaps you also worry about exposing yourself to criticism or rejection on the basis of your ideas, identity, background, or political beliefs. Such fears are legitimate, especially for those scholars who are already marginalized in the academy. Name these fears and acknowledge that you have a right to feel your anxieties. Then assess whether the actual risks are worth silencing yourself by not putting your work out there at all.

Try to reframe the editorial and publication process in your mind, thinking of it not as an adversarial set of gatekeeping encounters—though it can be that at times—but as a process designed to make your work the best it can be before it goes public. Your manuscript doesn't have to be perfect when entering the process, because you'll be taking it through several cycles of development before considering it to be finished. There will be multiple opportunities to improve it, and editors, peer reviewers, and supportive readers will be alongside to help.

Ultimately, you must choose a side in what Howard Becker calls "the tension between making it better and getting it done."[1] Take comfort in the fact that no text is flawless—even when it reaches the point of publication—because everyone involved in the publishing process is only human. Pull any published book off your shelf and assess it as a developmental editor would, as you've now learned how to do. You'll soon see that all books, even widely celebrated ones, leave opportunities on the table. The books were published because the authors were able to let them go.

Let your manuscript do its work. You can always write another one. This book will be here for you when you do.

ACKNOWLEDGMENTS

THIS BOOK could not exist without the hundreds of scholarly writers who have trusted me with their manuscripts and book proposals. I thank every author who has given me the opportunity to become a better developmental editor by engaging with their work. In particular, I recognize Helle Strandgaard Jensen, Oliver Haimson, Blake Atwood, and Lilly Irani, whose outstanding books I reference in this text.

My gratitude is also deep for the twenty writers who served as beta readers for this manuscript: Judith Babbitts, Amanda Boston, Collie Fulford, Jeanette Yih Harvie, Amber Hickey, Lucy Hinton, Lynn Mie Itagaki, Taryn D. Jordan, Harleen Kaur, Irina Kogan, Aynne Kokas, Rennie Lee, Lily Liang, Laura López-Sanders, Lexi Neame, crystal am nelson, Chika O. Okafor, Piyush Pushkar, Bryson White, and Hailee Yoshizaki-Gibbons. Their generous wisdom and enthusiasm gave me the confidence to finish and release this book, and it's much more useful due to their feedback. Elizabeth DeWolf, Steven E. Gump, Stephen B. Heard, and Jane Joann Jones served as friendly reviewers for the manuscript, and they, along with three anonymous reviewers secured by Princeton University Press, pushed this book in productive directions. I'd also like to thank the many academic editors and writers who have taken the time to answer my questions, share their working practices with me, or respond to my online posts. There are too many to name here individually, but please know that your insights have been informative and appreciated all along the way. Colin Campbell and Brad Waskewich helped me produce the images that appear in the book. The responsibility for any remaining shortcomings in this book lies with me.

I'm grateful to my publishing partners at Princeton University Press for their commitment to this project, including editor Matt Rohal (who never declined to get in a Zoom meeting with me when I had questions), assistant editor Alena Chekanov, contracts manager Ceylan Akturk, production editor Michelle Scott, manager of publishing operations partnerships Elizabeth Byrd, production manager Erin Suydam, creative director Maria Lindenfeldar, book and cover designer Karl Spurzem, illustration manager Dimitri Karetnikov, copyeditor Rebecca Faith, proofreader Juli Angel, indexer Mary Ann Lieser, copywriter David Campbell, marketing associate Steve Stillman, marketing manager Barbara Tonetti, promotions manager Maria Whelan, publicist Alyssa Sanford, digital production specialist Elizabeth Blazejewski, digital and audio publishers Danielle D'Orlando and Clare Ferris, social media manager Sydney Bartlett, Katie Stileman and Molly Grote with PUP Speaks, press director Christie Henry, and everyone else who has helped and will help this book find its readers. I also thank Peter Dougherty (now retired from Princeton UP) for giving *The Book Proposal Book* a chance as a founding title in the Skills for Scholars series. This book wouldn't have happened without that one.

For countless conversations, venting sessions, and distractions, I give thanks to Inna Arzumanova, Sarah Banet-Weiser, Michelle Boyd, Emily Campbell, John Cheney-Lippold, Zach Curd, Liz DeWolf, Christina Dunbar-Bester-Hester, Jane Joann Jones, Jenni Gritters, Jessica Kaufman, Betty Lai, Rebecca Marcum, Heather McCoy, Kate McKean, Meghan Moran, Zach Norton, and Evren Savcı. I've been buoyed by the moral support of all my family in New York and Michigan, especially Bill and Sally Waskewich and my dad, Willard Stacer. Thank you to my children for their patience and to the educators and childcare providers who kept them occupied, healthy, and happy while I worked on this book.

Finally, nothing at all would be possible, let alone writing this book, without Brad Waskewich's inexhaustible love and support. I can never thank you enough.

Checklist of Opportunities and Assessment Questions

THIS APPENDIX compiles all the development opportunities and accompanying assessment questions found in Chapters 4 through 7. As a reminder, opportunities marked with an asterisk are among the top ten most common areas for development I've encountered in scholarly book manuscripts as a developmental editor. Opportunities marked with a double asterisk are among the top five. This checklist can also be downloaded at https://manuscriptworks.com/book.

Opportunities to Develop Your Argument (Chapter 4)

____ Give your text an argument**

Does the text have a core argument?

Is the core argument stated directly near the beginning of the text?

____ Distinguish your main argument from subordinate arguments and other types of claims*

> If multiple arguments are competing for prominence, which argument is most pivotal?
>
> Can other arguments be nested below the main argument to support it, perhaps as chapter-level or section-level arguments?
>
> Can some arguments be labeled more accurately as premises, implications, exhortations, or claims for significance?
>
> Can some arguments be cut from the manuscript and repurposed elsewhere?

____ Make your argument portable*

> Is the manuscript's main argument constructed to be portable beyond its immediate research context?

____ Sharpen your argument by defining your main concepts*

> Are key concepts defined precisely enough?
>
> Are key concepts named explicitly throughout the text using consistent vocabulary?

____ Solidify your contribution by aligning the scope of your argument with the interests of your intended readers

> Is the scope of your main argument aligned with the interests of your intended readership?
>
> Is the manuscript's contribution explicitly articulated?

Opportunities to Develop Your Evidence
(Chapter 5)

____ Support all arguments with evidence**

Is each argument in the text directly supported by evidence?
Which arguments, if any, would be more convincing if
supported by additional evidence?
Is each piece of evidence explicitly connected to the text's
core argument or a sub-argument?
Should any evidence be located closer to the point it's
meant to support?

____ Provide only as much support as your arguments need

Is there more than enough evidence to support certain
points?
Is there any evidence that doesn't closely support an
argument?
Does the text include excessive evidence from the
scholarship of other writers?
Does the text include excessive discussion of methods and
methodology?
Could any of the excessive evidence be put to use elsewhere?

____ Present sufficient and reasonable analysis of all evidence*

Does each piece of evidence have corresponding analysis
that connects it to an argument?
Are long passages of primary source material accompanied
by, and possibly interwoven with, original analysis?
Is visual evidence described and interpreted appropriately
in the written text?
Is all analysis in the text logically sound?

Opportunities to Develop Your Structure
(Chapter 6)

____ Create a strong sense of narrative with your book's table of contents**

Is there an underlying narrative logic to the order of your
chapters?
Would this narrative logic be clear to readers?
Does each chapter have its own cohesive argument or
purpose in relation to the entire text?

____ Organize your material in a logical flow at the section and
paragraph level*

Does each piece of material have a purpose that serves the
chapter's argument and the manuscript's overall argument?
Does the order of your material help pull your reader
through the logic of your text at the section and
paragraph level?

____ Consider conventions when deciding how to organize
your book into parts

Do your body chapters function as self-contained units
with their own cohesive topics, evidence, and
sub-arguments?
Do your other chapter types also adhere to genre
expectations for scholarly books?
If you said no to either of the preceding questions, do you
have well-considered reasons for departing from
convention, and will those be clear to the reader?

____ Use titles, headings, and topic sentences to signal content
and purpose to the reader**

Do all units have descriptive titles, headings, or topic
   sentences?

Does the text's main title and subtitle clearly convey the
   topic of your manuscript as well as hint at your approach
   to the topic?

Does each chapter title clearly convey the topic and
   approach of the chapter?

Does each section heading clearly convey the topic and
   approach of the section?

Do you use topic sentences effectively throughout the text?

____ Use breaks and transitions to signal relationships between
parts of the text

Do breaks in your manuscript between chapters, sections,
   and paragraphs accurately signal shifts in topic or
   purpose?

Do you use transitional language to illuminate the
   relationship between material on either side of major
   breaks in the text?

____ Shorten or lengthen your text to align with reader needs
and publisher requirements

Is the total length of your manuscript on target for your
   intended publisher or norms in your field?

Are your chapter lengths consistent with norms in your
   field?

Are the lengths of component parts, such as chapters and
   sections within chapters, roughly equal to each other?

If you answered no to any of the preceding questions, do
   you have reasonable justification for departing from
   convention?

Opportunities to Develop Your Style
(Chapter 7)

____ Foreground your own ideas**

Do the words of others take up more space than your own
in any given paragraph or section of your manuscript?
When discussing the ideas of other scholars, do you always
make clear how they connect to your own points?
Are there any references to other scholarship that are no
longer necessary to include?

____ Make considered choices about notes

Do you take a coherent approach to notes across your
manuscript?
If you make extensive use of notes, is such an approach
necessary or advantageous in your field?

____ Strike a consistent and appropriate tone

Is your tone consistent throughout the text?
Is your tone appropriate for your intended readership?
Do you use vivid description and personal perspective
appropriately to forge a connection with your readers?

____ Clear up sentence-level obfuscations

Are your key points unencumbered by sentence-level
issues such as:
Specialist terminology?
Passive constructions?
Hedgy language?
Long or overly complex sentences?
Ambiguous pronouns?

Sample Editorial Materials

THE SAMPLE editorial materials in this appendix are based on a real scholarly manuscript that I worked on as a developmental editor with author Helle Strandgaard Jensen. Her book was published by Oxford University Press in 2023 under the title *Sesame Street: A Transnational History*. These materials are presented for illustrative purposes only, so that you can see concrete examples of how various steps in the manuscript development method might be applied to a real manuscript in progress. If you're intrigued by the content of Dr. Jensen's book, I encourage you to read the published version and cite it directly.

This appendix includes the following:

1. Two pages of the manuscript marked up during the assessment phase using the procedure described in Chapter 3
2. A structural chart of the manuscript's contents, outlined at the chapter level, as described in Chapter 6
3. A structural chart of one passage from the manuscript, outlined at the paragraph level, as described in Chapter 6
4. A sample editorial summary, as described in Chapter 8
5. Several pages of the manuscript with itemized edits indicated in the text, as described in Chapter 9

1. Marked-Up Text, Assessment Phase

CHAPTER 2

Ensuring Early Success: Strategies to Conquer the International Market

idea of Sesame Street as univers-ally appeal-ing

shocking quotation!!

EV

"We are like the British Empire. Someday the sun will never set on Sesame Street," Joan Ganz Cooney told the *New York Magazine* in April 1971. Cooney, the president of Children's Television Workshop had been the head of the organization from the very beginning and continued to be its public face. At this point in time, her dream of colonizing all the world's television sets with Bert, Ernie, and Big Bird seemed right on track. With fifty percent growth in sales of the English version from 1970 to 1971 and new foreign-language co-productions on the way, *Sesame Street* seemed unstoppable. What were the reasons for its rapid success internationally? In an interview given six months earlier, Cooney had explained quite clearly that there was "no question of [*Sesame Street's*] universality," because even when shown to children in India who had never seen any television before, it was a "smash hit." Sesame Street's innate ability to capture all preschoolers worldwide, simply because of its brilliance, was, and still is, a story often retold by the Workshop to explain it success. It was never considered that these children might have been fascinated by the idea of watching television and any program might have done the trick—or that the Workshop's intense marketing campaigns might had worked the wonders it had hoped for.

AN

safer to say "acknowl-edged," based on evidence available?

The Workshop's fixation with *Sesame Street*'s universal appeal fitted nicely with its rapid domestic success across a multitude of demographics. But attributing the worldwide breakthrough to its universal appeal obscured the vast efforts the Workshop put into making *Sesame Street* a globally recognized brand. This explanation not only downplayed all of the work, time, and money, it had poured into making *Sesame Street* a new standard for educational preschool television in the US; it also downplayed the vast resources deployed to persuade the rest of the world of this idea.

*

international appeal had to be fought for

Persuading foreign broadcasters to perceive *Sesame Street* as a new global standard for educational preschool programs was a highly demanding process. The Workshop understood that if it wanted to create a global hit, it had to spend time and money up front. Its success depended on regular and sustained exchange of programs, ideas, and people between the different contexts over time—just like in any other global transformation process. Money had to change hands, new ideas about education of preschoolers through television had to be spread, and overseas broadcasters had to be convinced to buy *Sesame Street*. In a year, from mid-1970 to mid-1971, it was in large part the Workshop's elaborate marketing strategy for *Sesame Street* that helped to establish the show as a challenge to existing expectations about what role television could fulfill in preschoolers' lives. The forceful promotion of the show ensured a high demand for their product.

*

43

FIGURE B.1. Marked-up text, assessment phase, page one

The time and resources the Workshop spend on becoming a global hit was not purely as a matter of choice. As we have seen in the previous chapter, its limited access to public resources in the long run meant the Workshop had to make money from sales of programs overseas, develop co-productions, and sell merchandise if further programming was to air in the US. To survive as a non-profit organization in the United States, and preserve the domestic image as anti-commercial, it had no choice but to try raise a profit by making *Sesame Street* a hit with children in places as far apart as Kenya, India, Mexico, and Japan. Something that required an aggressive sales strategy.

The Workshop's strategy was founded on a dual wish. It wanted to make sufficient revenue to fund future domestic English-language versions of *Sesame Street* and, at the same time, it wanted to preserve its integrity as a non-profit organization with an altruistic interest in advancing a new idea of educational television for preschoolers. It was difficult to combine international commercialization with the claim of domestic anti-commercialism. In the Workshop's archives, this is reflected in the hundreds of documents, many of which form the basis of this chapter, where it discussed this strategy of selling without appearing to sell and instructing the European sales agents exactly how to promote the show in the right way.

This chapter explores the early worldwide efforts to sell *Sesame Street*. The Workshop's global campaign for *Sesame Street* in 1970 and 1971 forms an essential backdrop for how the program was received in Europe, because even the transfer and demarcation in Europe that took place in national or regional settings, were highly affected by the Workshop's business model developed on a global scale. In my exploration of the early attempts to promote and sell *Sesame Street* both as an entirely new idea and as an alternative to existing preschool shows, the entanglement between personal networking and the Workshop's economic motivations will take center stage as this was a crucial interconnection for its international advancement.

Taking *Sesame Street* global called for a range of activities: It began with the German-based Prix Jeunesse Foundation whose festival and research activities that became an important transfer hub for *Sesame Street*, as the Workshop was very skilled in navigating the different opportunities it provided. From 1970 it included the hire sales agents that extended the Workshop's network in international broadcasting, both to sell the English-language version and to explore the feasibility of co-productions. Together the utilization of the international hub and the employment of agents were ways in which the Workshop labored to transform *Sesame Street* into a central reference point in the global production of television for young children—all unfolding in a worldwide market in which preschool television was a rising stock.

44

FIGURE B.2. Marked-up text, assessment phase, page two

2. Structural Chart, Chapter Level

TABLE B-1. Structural chart, chapter level

Page Range	Topic /Title	Purpose	Location Logic	Editorial Ideas
3–5	Preface	Walks the reader through my research process and reveals my ambivalence about the subject matter. Works to establish my expertise and prepares the reader for the book's controversial argument.	My tone is more direct here, almost confessional. This metacommentary makes sense to come at the beginning before the reader dives into the rest of the book.	N/A (no structural edits needed)
6–19	Introduction: A Transnational History of Childhood, Television, and Education	States the book's main argument that although the Children's Television Workshop (CTW, makers of *Sesame Street*) presented their program as a universally appealing cultural product for children, other countries didn't immediately accept the program because they saw it as heavily shaped by American ideologies of childhood, education, and commercial entertainment. To sell *Sesame Street* in other countries, which the show's business model depended on, the makers went to great lengths to convince national broadcasters around the world of the program's value and compatibility with local views about childhood, education, and the purpose of children's television. This chapter also articulates the book's intellectual contributions; establishes the book's scope, methods, methodological approach, and archive; and outlines the book's remaining chapters.	This introduction is necessary to bring the book's interdisciplinary readership up to speed on the historical context for *Sesame Street*'s development and international success and the various literatures underlying my intervention. This chapter also establishes my authority and the rigor of my research, preparing readers for the information they'll receive in the body chapters.	N/A

Page Range	Topic / Title	Purpose	Location Logic	Editorial Ideas
20–42	No Amateursville: The Workshop's Business Model	Describes how *Sesame Street* was created in the US and sketches the political, economic, and cultural conditions underlying the show's development. Exposes the ideological biases and power relations that were baked into *Sesame Street* from the start, characterizing the show as aligned with conservative, positivistic ideas of child development and education while cultivating a progressive brand identity (which was central to the show's success with parents and funders). Reveals how the Children's Television Workshop were dismissive of criticisms that questioned the program's core values.	This chapter is necessary to establish *Sesame Street*'s distinctively American flavor, as context for why the show wasn't automatically accepted in other countries and in fact required a great deal of active selling by the Children's Television Workshop. These sales efforts will be documented in the remaining chapters. This chapter also explains why the CTW relied on the international sales of the show that will be discussed in later chapters: the public television model used in the US wasn't ultimately sustainable, though it was core to the show's domestic brand identity as public service television.	N/A
43–68	Ensuring Early Success: Strategies to Conquer the International Market	Gives an overview of the elaborate, carefully controlled marketing efforts the Children's Television Workshop employed to establish *Sesame Street* as a strong brand in foreign markets. Provides extensive evidence to contradict the CTW's consistent public claims that cultural transfer of *Sesame Street* was automatic due to the universal appeal of the program to children around the world.	This chapter builds on the previous chapter by offering further evidence of the CTW's sales approach. It also offers global examples of processes that readers will see happen in later chapters in specific European national contexts.	Bring all material about France into this chapter (some of it is currently in Chapter 4).

(continued)

Page Range	Topic /Title	Purpose	Location Logic	Editorial Ideas
69–98	Ban and Bother: The Workshop's Troubles in the UK	Documents the struggles the CTW faced in bridging incompatibilities between the CTW's approach in *Sesame Street*, the UK broadcasting landscape, and British views on how children should be educated in their preschool years. This chapter shows how local cultural and market conditions in a specific place were an obstacle to the cultural transfer of a product whose makers were unaware of or uninterested in local traditions.	This is the first body chapter to cover a national case study. It narrows the narrative scope of the previous chapter, which provided a broad overview of international sales efforts. It makes sense to begin the three case study chapters with this case, because the CTW saw the UK as a very important market and saw the BBC as a gateway to broadcasters in the rest of Europe (which the next two chapters will cover). This chapter marks a narrative turning point in the book as we start to see the CTW's approach to selling *Sesame Street* fail due to the CTW's insensitivity to local conditions.	N/A
99–134	*Sesame Street* in West Germany, France and Italy: Negotiating the Needs of Local Markets	This chapter shows how the CTW navigated local production and adaptations in non-English-speaking contexts, revealing the lengths the CTW had to go to in accommodating localized versions of *Sesame Street* while staying true to the show's established brand.	This chapter reinforces the book's main argument, while adding a layer of complexity to the previous case study by discussing versions of Sesame Street that were sold in languages other than English.	The section on the Open Sesame model of coproduction developed in France with *Bonjour Sesame* could be useful in Chapter 2, since this model was widely used around the world and would be helpful for readers in understanding the CTW's overall global

Page Range	Topic /Title	Purpose	Location Logic	Editorial Ideas
				strategy (which is the topic of Chapter 2). The section of this chapter on Italy could also probably be heavily condensed so that this chapter focuses mainly on the West Germany case.
135–158	Other Childhoods: *Sesame Street* in Scandinavia	Depicts the CTW's unsuccessful attempt to sell *Sesame Street* in Denmark, Norway, and Sweden. The cultural values and views of appropriate educational material and children's television programming in the US and Scandinavia were so incompatible that co-productions of *Sesame Street* were ultimately impossible to negotiate. Gives definitive proof that the CTW's frequent claims about the universal appeal of *Sesame Street* were false.	This chapter provides the starkest case study of the book's main argument, so it makes sense to come as the culmination of the book's previous body chapters.	N/A
159–168	Narrow Vision: Looking Back at a Global Success	This chapter looks at how the cultural transfer of *Sesame Street* has been interpreted in hindsight by the CTW and others. It also examines the implications of the evidence from previous chapters to provide commentary on American liberalism and cultural diplomacy writ large.	This chapter should come after the case study chapters because it synthesizes the findings in those chapters and provides a strongly stated interpretation. This chapter builds on a different kind of evidence than the previous chapters in that it focuses on the CTW's attempts to control the narrative of its activities rather than documenting the	The distinct shift in tone and scope could make this chapter feel jarring to readers. Because my voice is stronger in this chapter, and the topic is more meta, it might make sense to label this chapter as a conclusion rather than a regular body chapter. But I will have to figure out what to do with the existing conclusion.

(continued)

Page Range	Topic / Title	Purpose	Location Logic	Editorial Ideas
			activities themselves, as previous chapters did. Therefore, it's logical to present this chapter in its current position, outside the arc of the case study chapters.	
169–175	Conclusion: Noble Intentions and Cultural Clashes	This short chapter summarizes the findings of the previous chapters.	As a summary of points previously made, this material makes sense to appear at the end of the book.	Because this chapter repeats points made in the previous chapter, this chapter could be folded into the previous chapter, which I also thought could become a conclusion. Some of the summary in this chapter could be heavily condensed too.
176–177	List of Consulted Archival Material	Documents all evidence drawn on in the book. This is important because I'm making claims that could be controversial and that my subject (the CTW) might wish to deny, based on their previous attempts to control the narrative and brand identity of *Sesame Street*.	Logical for this to come at the end of the book, after the narrative chapters but before the endnotes.	N/A

3. Structural Chart, Paragraph Level

TABLE B-2. Structural chart, paragraph level

Page Range	Topic	Purpose	Location Logic	Editorial Ideas
100–101	West Germany becomes interested in preschool education in the 1960s	Sets stage for West Germany developing educational children's television.	Comes at the beginning of the West Germany case study because it establishes why this national context could have been a good fit for *Sesame Street*.	N/A
101	West Germany's ideologies of child development were rooted in continental philosophy in contrast to US ideologies which were rooted in cognitive psychology.	Shows that although both US and West Germany valued preschool education, they had opposing approaches.	Provides context for the conflicts that would arise between the US makers of *Sesame Street* (the Children's Television Workshop, CTW) and local West German television producers.	N/A
101–102	West Germany saw preschool education as playing an important role in child development.	Shows that cultural conditions in West Germany were friendly to educational children's television programming.	Establishes why this national context could have been a good fit for *Sesame Street*.	Same purpose as passage above. Should be folded into the earlier passage and trimmed for repetition.
102–103	Existing children's programming on two West German networks.	Illustrates how West German ideas about child development and preschool education were integrated into their television programming.	Sets up a contrast with the kind of content the CTW favored.	N/A

(continued)

TABLE B-2. (*continued*)

Page Range	Topic	Purpose	Location Logic	Editorial Ideas
103	The CTW arrives at a time when West German networks were interested in developing children's programming.	Shows that the CTW and West German networks were both invested in children's educational television.	Reiterates that this national context could be a good fit for *Sesame Street*.	Similar point as two passages above. Consider combining.
103	West German TV networks formed a preschool programming working group which discussed *Sesame Street*.	Shows that West German networks were supportive of children's educational TV programming in general and *Sesame Street* in particular.	Expands on points made above with concrete evidence that West Germany could have been a receptive context for *Sesame Street*.	Should follow previous passages (as it currently does) but shouldn't be separated by a new section heading (as in current draft).

4. Editorial Summary

What follows is a modified version of the editorial summary I wrote as Dr. Jensen's developmental editor. I've rewritten this hypothetical version from Dr. Jensen's own point of view, as if she had used the manuscript development method from this book on her own text, to illustrate both how you might structure your own editorial summary and the kinds of things you might include.

As you read, keep in mind that your own editorial summary might vary in a number of ways. Dr. Jensen's manuscript was at a late stage of development when this summary was written. The manuscript had already been through peer review successfully, and the author was preparing the final version of the manuscript to go into production. It therefore didn't need drastic development with respect to its argument or overall structure. I tried to provide a good amount of detail here and write in complete sentences so that the summary would read coherently to you. But if you were writing a summary for yourself, you might use more shorthand language and bullet points. As always, use this sample as inspiration but feel free to find the application of the method that works best for you.

EDITORIAL SUMMARY FOR
SELLING SESAME STREET ABROAD
MARCH 2022

Major parameters of the manuscript

Topic

- How the Children's Television Workshop tried to sell *Sesame Street* around the world and the resistance it faced in local contexts

Scope

- Examines the earliest efforts to sell *Sesame Street* outside the US in the late 1960s and 1970s; considers worldwide efforts but provides the most detail about cases in Western Europe: the UK, West Germany, France, Italy, Denmark, Norway, and Sweden

Approach

- Historical/archival methods
- Critical cultural studies analytical framework

- In conversation with scholarship on childhood, children's media, education, cultural transfer, and new global history

Overall purpose

- The book establishes that the makers of *Sesame Street* believed—or at least very much represented themselves as believing—that their show was a universally appealing cultural product for children that would be smoothly accepted everywhere. Yet the realities of their attempts to sell *Sesame Street* abroad tell a more complicated story. Contrary to the Children's Television Workshop's claims of "culture-free TV," I explain how the show was heavily shaped by distinctly American assumptions about childhood, education, and commercial entertainment.
- I want to tell a story about *Sesame Street* that complicates the narrative that has been advanced, quite strategically, by the program's makers, and in doing so make a broader point about the transnational transfer of cultural products into local contexts where American ideologies about childhood, education, and the purpose of children's television aren't dominant.

Goals and intended readerships

- The book is under contract and the full manuscript has been peer reviewed. I'm now preparing the final version to go into production.
- I hope to reach interdisciplinary scholarly readers who are interested in the history of childhood, education, media, and transnational cultural transfer.

- I also really want this book to reach readers outside of academia who are open to a critical take on American culture and *Sesame Street* in particular.
- I want to shape public conversation about children's media.
- Revisions at this stage are aimed at making the narrative compelling and the arguments understandable for a wide scholarly and non-scholarly audience.

Feedback to be addressed

- My total word limit is 100,000 and I'm about 10,000 over that now. Cuts are needed.
- One peer reviewer wanted to see more description of European preschool programming; I've already added a discussion of this to Chapter 1, but I borrowed some of that discussion from Chapter 5, so I need to decide where it should ultimately go.
- One peer reviewer wanted to see more discussion of the BBC as an exporter of children's programming. I've already added a few sentences on this in Chapter 3.

Argument

The main argument of the book is that, had *Sesame Street* been as universally appealing as the CTW claimed it was, it would have been accepted in foreign contexts with little effort needed by the CTW. Yet the CTW went to great lengths to make the show accepted in countries where domestic cultural values clashed with the American values that were baked into *Sesame Street*'s concept from the start. The CTW's long-standing narrative of itself and its show is therefore flawed, maybe even dishonest. The larger takeaway from this study is that there is no such thing as "culture-free TV," and the process of international transfer of cultural products is never straightforward or independent of power relations.

This is a strong argument, solidly reinforced throughout the book. Although the book's scope is the history of one specific program, the dynamics documented are more broadly portable, especially for cultural theorists who might be looking at transnational cultural transfer in different times and locations.

I could be clearer about the conceptual lessons I want readers to take from each of the specific case study chapters (UK, West Germany, Scandinavia). The history and local conditions in each case are well presented, but I could provide more conceptual framing by adding a few sentences near the beginning of each of those chapters. This framing will make the later chapters of the book even more useful to instructors and students of cultural studies.

I'd like to expand on the brief argument I make about American liberalism in Chapters 2 and 6. Doing so will help my book converse more directly with the literature on Americanization, cultural diplomacy, and the legacy of Cold War culture, which will broaden the readership, especially among historians. I think I can make this argument more prominent by turning Chapter 6 into a conclusion and centering the liberalism argument there. This will have the added benefit of making the book's conclusion more exciting, as the current conclusion chapter is mostly summary and is very short.

Evidence

In general, my claims are thoroughly supported by archival evidence, which I've documented meticulously. I want to be very careful about backing up all claims because I'm concerned about being accused of unfairness toward *Sesame Street* and the

CTW. The general public tends to feel quite positively about *Sesame Street*, and I want readers to understand my points without writing me off as an unfair critic.

More direct quotation from my archival sources will also be helpful in a few places, to "show my work" to the reader as to how I arrived at my claims based on the evidence available. For example, when explaining Cooney's views of how television should be used to provide preschool education (pp. 23–26), I could quote directly from her 1966 study to support my characterizations. I could pull back on my interpretations of feelings or intent on the part of CTW personnel in a few places, since such claims are hard to prove based on the archival evidence I had access to. As I revise, I'll make sure to present what people actually said or wrote in order to make my points and let readers draw their own conclusions about intent.

Some details I found in my archival research can be trimmed during revision, especially in chapters that are running long and where the narrative can be tightened to more closely track with the chapter-level argument. For example, in the discussion of how *Sesame Street* was sold in France, I've included details about interpersonal conflict and the development of the French pilot that aren't entirely necessary for readers to understand the broader points I want to make. The stories are interesting, but because I also have to reduce length, I have to be choosy about which incidents I describe in detail.

Structure

ORGANIZATION

The manuscript doesn't require major structural changes. The current table of contents can remain largely the same with respect to chapter divisions, except for combining the current Chapter 6 with the current conclusion to form one somewhat longer conclusion chapter. Some material in Chapter 4 on France and *Bonjour Sesame* as an example of the Open Sesame model could be moved up to Chapter 2 to tell a more cohesive story about the CTW's overall efforts at gaining a foothold in foreign markets.

Light reorganizing in specific chapters could be helpful; see individual chapter plans below.

SIGNALING

The book's title could possibly be tightened from the current *Selling Sesame Street Abroad* to *Selling Sesame Street*. The shorter title is punchier and also encompasses the points I make in Chapter 1 about the CTW's domestic sales strategy in the US and in Chapter 6 about the CTW's narrative of itself, which is also a kind of "selling."

The current subtitle could also be altered slightly from *A History of Childhood, Education, and the Cultural Resistance Towards the Show* to *A Transnational History of Childhood, Education, and Cultural Resistance*. The new version is a bit more encompassing and subtly hints that this story of cultural transfer and resistance transcends what happened with one particular program. Putting "transnational" in the subtitle would also make up for removing "abroad" from the main title.

My chapter titles and headings largely work to orient readers to the points I want to make. In a few cases (introduction, Chapter 1) I can be clearer about the conceptual contributions of the chapters and their purpose in the book's larger narrative. See individual chapter plans below for thoughts on new chapter titles. I'll also check my section headings as I revise to make sure they signal takeaways in addition to topics. My topic sentences are strong.

In a few cases, sections that cover similar ground can be combined and trimmed of repetitive material. Long paragraphs can be broken up so that each point gets its due treatment.

LENGTH

The total length is about 10,000 words over the limit in my contract (100,000 words). I may be able to submit a version that is 4,000 or 5,000 words over, but I want to add material to Chapter 6, which will become the conclusion, so I need to cut elsewhere.

Here are the respective lengths of my chapters currently:

Preface—1,560 words
Introduction—9,081 words
Chapter 1—14,168 words
Chapter 2—16,076 words
Chapter 3—19,499 words
Chapter 4—22,425 words
Chapter 5—14,577 words
Chapter 6—6, 367 words
Conclusion—3,824 words

These totals are inclusive of notes. The chapter lengths mostly feel appropriate for my field, especially because of the extensive documentation of sources in the notes.

Chapter 4 is the outlier in terms of length and is probably at least 5,000 words too long, so cutting significant length there will be a big help in getting the total length of the manuscript down. I will also be cutting large portions of the Conclusion when I combine it with Chapter 6, so that should get the total length to a good place. See individual chapter plans below for specifics.

I will look for additional places to trim repetition throughout the manuscript.

Style

My voice is strong throughout the book. I cite other scholarship to support my approach, but mostly in the introduction. I could stand to add a few more citations to the literature on new global history and previous studies of *Sesame Street* and the CTW in the intro.

The body chapters are almost entirely composed of original research and interpretation; my voice comes across clearly there. The preface is quite personal, and I hope it will help readers understand where I'm coming from in my critique of a beloved cultural product.

The notes document the archival evidence I rely on in the text, in conjunction with an appendix that lists all consulted archival material. The current draft has footnotes because they are easier to work with as I rewrite and restructure the manuscript, but they will become endnotes in the final version so as not to clutter the main text.

My tone is largely consistent throughout. This book is unavoidably critical of the CTW, but I've made an effort to strike a neutral tone with respect to the Workshop and present their activities as supported by the evidence. The one place where my tone comes across as especially critical is in Chapter 6, where I discuss the CTW's attempts to control the public narrative of its activities, in contrast to previous chapters which were largely focused on documenting the activities themselves. In order to persuade the readers I want to reach, who may be coming from a position of unexamined bias *toward* the CTW, I want to make sure my tone doesn't alienate. However, if I combine Chapter 6 with my current conclusion, I think it's okay if the tone feels a bit less neutral than in the rest of the book. Readers expect the author's voice to come across more strongly in a book's conclusion.

Reviewer 2 noted grammatical issues across the text, but I don't think they interfere with meaning. I'll be handling the language editing with the publisher later on. We'll begin with one chapter so I can approve the style and degree of editing done by the copyeditor; then the rest of the manuscript will be copyedited to that standard.

Notes on Individual Chapters

PREFACE

The purpose here is to walk the reader through my research process and my own ambivalence toward my subject matter. I'm trying to prepare the reader for my provocative argument and establish a personal connection before they get into the book. I believe the current draft is effective and no major changes are needed.

INTRODUCTION

This chapter also feels solid. I've tried to engage the reader with approachable storytelling and a traditional structure for an introduction. I could emphasize the book's conceptual contributions a bit more and provide additional explanation of the scholarly frameworks I'm drawing on, such as new global history.

The current title of the introduction is repetitive with the book's main title. It would be good to give it a more specific title to introduce the book's argument. I could change the intro title to "Culture-Free TV?" (which I found during my archival research and had at one time considered for the book's main title). It's an evocative, pithy phrase that pierces the problem at the heart of the whole book.

CHAPTER 1

This chapter shows who produced *Sesame Street* and under what conditions in order to expose the ideological biases and power relations that were baked into the program from the start. Even fans of the show who think they know *Sesame Street* well will learn a lot here and have their eyes opened to dynamics of which they were likely previously unaware. This chapter reinforces the scope of the book's concern: the day-to-day production context of *Sesame Street* and how that production context shaped the show's content and its later cultural transfer outside the US. This chapter also sets up the core characterizations I want readers to associate with the show:

- conservative, positivist ideologies of child development, education, and opportunity
- commercial and entertainment logics
- the centrality of *Sesame Street*'s brand image to its funding both domestically and abroad

The chapter explains the roots of *Sesame Street*'s premise in the field of cognitive psychology and discusses how the Workshop actively consolidated their particular ideology of children's needs.

This chapter could be streamlined to reduce repetition and unnecessary detail. Specifically, the material on pages 29 and 30 that delves into the Workshop's efforts to focus on "formal, non-controversial education" as part of its need to cultivate an image that pleased parents and funders could be integrated into the later section (heading: "Making a business of keeping funders, parents and the middle class happy," pp. 34–38) since these two passages cover similar ground. The final section (pp. 39–42) could also be significantly reduced in length, essentially becoming one or two concluding paragraphs at the end of the previous section. The one paragraph on the "schedule approach" in European television may be useful to move into the book's introduction chapter. The discussion of *Play Room* can wait until Chapter 5.

Because this chapter sets up themes that will appear later in the book—such as the Workshop's aim of closing the achievement gap between privileged and underprivileged children and the Workshop's sensitivity to outside criticism—it will be important to make sure the significance of each theme is properly established in this chapter. I'll add a few sentences to the relevant sections in order to make sure readers understand why the material is significant.

The current title of this chapter ("No Amateursville: The Workshop's Business Model") might be too obscure for readers to understand the main contributions this chapter is making. Something like "A Highly Controlled Experiment: The Workshop's Business Model" would get at the message of the chapter better. "Domestic Origins: The Workshop's Business Model" could also work as a straightforward description of the chapter's purpose in the overall narrative of the book.

CHAPTER 2

The purpose of this chapter is to dig deeper into the processes by which the Workshop introduced *Sesame Street* into foreign markets. I want readers to understand that this process was labor intensive, contrary to the Workshop's claims that they simply sold the show when they were approached, and that part of what made it labor intensive was the need to overcome objections to the show that stemmed from cultural differences in foreign contexts. The Workshop wasn't happy to let foreign broadcasters adapt the show as they saw fit, because the Workshop felt that strict control over their brand was necessary for the show's continued success.

This chapter also gives readers a sense of how precisely the show ended up being sold for broadcast abroad. I explain the foothold strategy and how the Workshop tried to get the US English-language version into as many markets as possible, even at a short-term financial loss, because their long-term strategy relied on universal brand recognition. I describe the general strategy of developing co-productions, which previews the following chapters where I'll dig into co-productions in specific national contexts.

This chapter begins to describe the Workshop's approach to a French co-production (pp. 58–67), but the story is unfinished here. It gets resolved later, in Chapter 4 (pp. 124–130). To reduce length in Chapter 4 and keep the story in this chapter cohesive, it makes sense to move all the French material into this chapter. This material can then be condensed to focus on only the key conceptual points I need readers to understand. In particular, I'll emphasize how the Workshop used the Open Sesame model when developing the French co-production *Bonjour Sesame*, because the Open Sesame model is key for readers to understand the Workshop's approach in Latin America and other regions that I don't cover in as much depth in the book.

CHAPTER 3

This chapter tells the story of attempted transfer of *Sesame Street* to the UK. This chapter doesn't need any significant revisions, although I could better set up the broader takeaways I want readers to get from this case study, connecting the chapter back to the book's overall contribution about cultural transfer. This can be done with just a few new sentences toward the beginning of the chapter.

I could also trim length in this chapter where I discuss US press coverage of the BBC's decision (pp. 84–88). This material is interesting and would be worth keeping if length wasn't a concern, but this chapter is a bit longer than the others and the overall length of the manuscript needs to be reduced. The material isn't strictly necessary to make the main point I want to make in this chapter.

CHAPTER 4

This chapter feels solid and doesn't necessarily require major changes to the content, but it's quite long at over 22,000 words. I don't strictly need the material on France and Italy, because the discussion of West Germany makes the chapter's point well enough on its own. Some of the material on France can be moved into Chapter 2 and condensed (as noted above). I can give a high-level gloss of the Workshop's strategy and outcomes in Italy in a paragraph or two, or cut Italy from the book entirely. The Italy material does fit with the book's argument, but the other cases make enough sense without discussing Italy. Again, this material would be fine to keep if I had the space for it, but I have to reduce length.

CHAPTER 5

This chapter on the transfer of *Sesame Street* to Scandinavia is in excellent shape. No major edits are needed.

CHAPTER 6

I plan to reframe Chapter 6 as the book's conclusion as noted above. The current conclusion draft is mostly unnecessary summary of the previous chapters. This material can be condensed down to a few paragraphs and used as the closing paragraphs of the new conclusion chapter. I'll indicate the specific edits needed with embedded notes in the manuscript.

Next Steps

Begin with major edits related to content and structure:

- Move material on France from Chapter 4 to Chapter 2
- Condense material on Italy in Chapter 4 to one or two paragraphs, or remove entirely
- Expand discussion of American liberalism in the current Chapter 6
- Condense material in the current conclusion down to a few paragraphs, removing most of the material that summarizes the book
- Put condensed conclusion paragraphs at the end of Chapter 6, which will become the new conclusion

Then handle less pressing content and structure edits:

- Trim detailed discussions that aren't necessary to convey main points, especially in Chapter 3 and in the material on France that got moved from Chapter 4 to Chapter 2
- Eliminate repetition by combining sections that cover similar ground, especially in Chapter 1
- Condense repetitive paragraphs across the manuscript

Then make brief additions of evidence and framing:

- Insert more direct quotation throughout the manuscript to support claims based on archival evidence
- Add citations on new global history to introduction
- Add a few sentences of clearer conceptual framing to the introduction, individual sections of Chapter 1, and at the beginnings of Chapters 3, 4, and 5

Finally, take care of signaling and stylistic matters:

- Break up long paragraphs
- Check for good topic sentences and section headings after all structural edits are complete and revise as needed
- Revise book title and titles of the introduction and Chapter 1
- Convert footnotes to endnotes

5. Itemized Edits

and the Workshop, both in terms of preschool education and in terms of measuring success, shaped the making of the West German version of *Sesame Street*.

In contrast to West Germany, conflicts of this sort are less evident in the scarce sources preserved from the Workshop's early business dealings in France and Italy. Furthermore, limited scholarly interest in the history of children's television in the two countries when compared with West Germany, Scandinavia and Britain adds to the difficulties of drawing comparative conclusions between the three countries considered in this chapter. Still, the sources that are preserved, notably in the Workshop's own archives and printed material from the period, provide insights into the localization of *Sesame Street* in France and Italy in the 1970s.

The Workshop had good reasons to seek a foothold in all three countries when they began to pursue foreign sales. France, West Germany and Italy were the three markets with most television sets in the World outside the Anglosphere and had well-established, national public service broadcasters. However, despite all being based in Western Europe there were vast differences in their programming for preschoolers and the ways in which these programs were structured and funded. The Workshop approached them very differently at first, not yet having developed a coherent marketing strategy. This chapter investigates the implications of these differences for the Workshop's success in selling their show as well as the response to local adaptation in the three countries. The West German case makes up the majority of the chapter. Not only was the Workshop the most successful, West German sources concerning localization are also the most plentiful.

The generic, 'language versions' that the Workshop had hoped to produce in France and West Germany and distribute to other places speaking these language (discussed in chapter two) turned out to be difficult. However, based on its experiences in the two countries, the Workshop developed several other modes of making the show available in Europe that it would later use elsewhere. For instance, to meet localization demands by French and West Germany broadcasters the Workshop needed to change the length of the show and definitions of what it meant to adapt it to other cultures. A new format for a 'cheap' adaptation was first sold to France and later fitted into a general model that could be reused on other markets including Italy, Spain, Portugal, Belgium and Sweden. The adaptation in West Germany was made on top of the experiences the Workshop made about this time in Latin American and then processed into a general framework for co-productions, which it also tried to use in Scandinavia. Understanding how local adaptations unfolded in specific contexts but was then later recycled in others provides valuable insight into how the Workshop's model for foreign sales was developed and the consequences of these for the localizations that followed.

WEST GERMANY

(handwritten note:) ☞ You don't need this broad heading, since the whole chapter will be refocused on W. Germany. Write new, descriptive heading for this section.

In West Germany, as elsewhere in Europe, there had been an increased in interest in the lives of young children and preschool provision throughout the 1960s. Inspired by new theories in child psychology that brought attention to the early lives of children and its possible impact on their later life, pedagogues, sociologists,

100

FIGURE B.3. Itemized edits embedded in the text, page one

nursery teachers and public intellectuals discussed how to best to help children. In West Germany much of this effort was concentrated on deliberations on how to make children self-aware, how to stimulate their creativity, independence and inspire a thirst for knowledge and social understanding. The German interest in early childhood development and education was, like in the US, aimed to understand how the child's social environment effected its intelligence and aptitude. However, unlike in the American cognitive psychology tradition that had inspired *Sesame Street*, the West German discussions were rooted in a long tradition of pedagogy linked to continental philosophy. This meant that rather than using data collection and manipulation to solve a possible gap in achievements and social inequality via cognitive skills training as in Sesame Street, the dominant West German solution found answers in qualitative, analytical approaches, similar to what took place in a British context. Here the way to a better, more educated and equal society was in the progressive milieus that influenced broadcasting for children sought in so-called 'emancipatory education.' This term has overlaps with what is called 'progressive education' in the Anglosphere. Thus, even if the educational psychology that had inspired *Sesame Street*'s philosophy and German psychology and education theory both offered ways of using preschool education to change the lives of the nation's citizens for the better, they represented two opposing approaches to how this improvement should happen. The Workshop took a compensatory approach— wanting children that lacked behind to catch up to their peers by intellectual stimulation by creating equality of opportunity. The idea of creating equality of opportunity through the educational system was also popular in West Germany, but it was mixed with an emancipatory approach—wanting all children to understand, navigate and possibly also question the norms and rules of adult-driven society. The latter focus on antiauthoritarianism was more pronounced in the German case than in the British, where a child-centered approach in television did not seem to equal a questioning of adult behavior and society to as large an extent as in West Germany.

Despite these differences between the approach of the Workshop and those favored in a German and British context, both traditions focused on early child development and how preschool education might shape it. Both groups believed that getting early childhood stimulation right was not only of crucial importance to the individual child, but also for its contribution to a modern, complex society with a high demand for a skilled labor force and increased welfare for all citizens. Like elsewhere in Europe, this resulted in discussions of the need for structured and regular preschool education in West Germany. "Pre-school education [was] a magic word" as two German academics later wrote about the period when *Sesame Street* was first shown to a West German audience. The renewed emphasis on preschool education, even if this education contrasted with *Sesame Street*'s cognitive skills training, prepared the ground for a new interest in broadcasting for preschoolers as a way to reach all young children with the stimulus they needed.

Television for young children had been limited in West Germany throughout the 1960s. The protection of small children from audiovisual material was most visible with the 1957 law that banned children under six from going to the cinema, but nationwide television networks had followed suit and only broadcasted programs

FIGURE B.4. Itemized edits embedded in the text, page two

for children 8 years and up until the end of the 1960s. Watching television was framed as a problematic activity that was portrayed as keeping children away from active use of their bodies and creativity. However the at end of the 1960s the interest in preschool education coincided with the growing realization of German parents and television producers that this now decades-old medium was part of small children's everyday life and routines even if it was not supposed to be so. This meant that at the very end of the 1960s West German attitudes towards preschool television changed. The argument was that if young children watched television they needed shows that were appropriate for their age group and that would help their enculturation process. The interest in preschool television was evident in both networks that covered West Germany.

The Zweites Deutsches Fernsehen (ZDF) network established in 1963, which covered all of West Germany with programming on Channel 2, in 1970 considered establishing a preschool program based on ideas from the BBC's *Playschool*. The other, older West German network. Arbeitsgemeinschaft der öffentlich-rechtlichen Rundfunkanstalten der Bundesrepublik Deutschland (ARD) consisted of nine independent regional corporations covering the countries' nine states with a mixture of joint and local programming on two channels (one for national viewing on Channel 1, the other for regional programming on Channel 3) The first program on ADR's network for preschoolers aired in 1969. It was made by the broadcasting corporation in Munich for a national audience. Thought the program was not related to the BBC's production, it had the same title albeit, of course, in German *Die Spielschule* (*The Play School*). *Die Spielschule* had a total of 13 episodes typical of the experimental, shorter formats of children's shows on public service broradcasters.

[ILLUSTRATION: map of Germany w. East and West as well as
West German broadcasting regions and broadcaster names]

The ideas for Die Spielschule had been discussed since 1967. The show was based on the ideas of emancipatory education. as it was aimed at giving the young viewers a very matter-of-fact impression of West German society and everyday life. It was also supposed to pose questions that would challenge commonly assumed self-evident facts and rules of the everyday lives of adults and children. and thereby take seriously children's perspectives. Consequently, the show had no studio recordings (or fixed location) was largely non-verbal. and made to be 'observed' to encourage children to draw their own conclusions about what they saw. Even if it was the regional ARD corporation in Munich that first made a preschool program, the area had gained attention network-wide. Several initiatives were taken to support the production of these programs. including research and a network-wide working group. From 1970 onwards. 30 minutes weekly for the national broadcast on was set aside on the network's Channel 1 that covered the entire country, for regionally produced programs to be broadcasted nationally. This meant that *Die Spielschule* was aired nation-wide and joined by preschool productions from the regional broadcasting corporations in West Berlin (*Kwatschnich*) and Cologne (*Sach und*

[handwritten margin note: This paragraph also feels repetitive Cut down and merge with first paragraph of this section. Distill to the main point.]

FIGURE B.5. Itemized edits embedded in the text, page three

Lachgeschichten) in 1970.

Though based on a very different approach to preschool education that the West German, *Sesame Street* arrived just in time to be part of the debate of what television for this age group should offer. Joan Ganz Cooney had already (in 1968) published her article about the Workshop's project in the internationally distributed. German-language journal, *Fernsehen und Bildung* and *Sesame Street* won the Prix Jeunesse Prize in 1970 at the international festival in Munich, an event attend by all of the most influential West German children's television producers. The exposure of the program as well as the Workshop's Paris-based agents' sales efforts had led to interest from both West German networks, ARD and ZDF. However, ZDF was, as said, also considering co-producing BBC's *Play School* as a better fit for the West German view of preschool education.

[handwritten margin note: You could remove this subheading and merge the two sections. They are making similar points.]

ARD's joint working group on preschool television

In early 1971, a joint ARD working group with representatives from all of its nine regional broadcasting companies had been established to develop preschool programming. As an official group that included all of ARD's nine broadcasting corporations, it became important for the development and expansion of preschool programs in West Germany. The group was expected to follow a policy proposal that outlined plans for child and family programming. The policy proposal that laid the foundation for the group demonstrates the high degree to which *Sesame Street* influenced the ARD's internal debate about preschool programming. Its third point explicitly mentions *Sesame Street* and offers a positive assessment of its approach to teaching:

"Particularly with a program for small children, it must be taken into account that experience has shown that the attractiveness of a television program suffers if the medium is understood purely as a means of conveying teaching material, neglecting the entertainment and playful elements. Even if the concept of "Sesame Street" cannot simply be transferred to a German context, the design of the series shows that a program can manage without obtrusive teaching, despite its fixed learning objectives, and can indeed be extremely attractive."

Thus, even if there were diverging attitudes towards *Sesame Street* within the Working Group, there was an agreement that *Sesame Street* offered an alternative to didacticism. The policy proposal was equally sympathetic to another feature of *Sesame Street*—need to fill a void for those children that were not able to attend preschool. The proposal also explicitly stated how preschool programs might help eliminate socio-cultural inequalities by filling out "a compensatory function to adjust educational opportunities," exactly as it was wished for *Sesame Street* to have in the US.

However, not everything about *Sesame Street* was seen as ideal or transferable to a West German context. The proposed policy clearly stated that programs should not focus on "one-sided promotion of the cognitive domain [but instead] aim at the overall development of the child, who should become aware of the world as it is." Instead of cognitive skills, the proposal called for programs that stimulated children creatively, socially and linguistically. Though the proposal clearly drew inspiration

FIGURE B.6. Itemized edits embedded in the text, page four

Supportive Readers in Manuscript Development

WHEN YOU complete each rotation through the manuscript development cycle, you'll have two possible paths forward. You can either try to take your manuscript to the next stage of the process with your chosen publisher or repeat the development cycle again. If your edits have changed the text substantially, it might be a good idea to do another quick cycle on your own, reassessing your text in its new form and making any changes that are still needed. However, don't get stuck in an endless loop of manuscript development. To be certain that your manuscript is able to do the work you need it to do, you'll have to let other people read it and see what happens.

You can get valuable feedback on whether your manuscript is working from the submission and peer review process. However, you may want to seek feedback from a set of people I call supportive readers before subjecting your manuscript to high-stakes evaluation. You may also want to get input from supportive readers before submitting the final version of your text for production. I call these external readers supportive, not because they are predisposed to think your manuscript is in great shape and only tell you nice things about it, but because they're willing to read your work to help you improve it. They may have feedback that's tough for you to hear, but they're willing to share it with you in time for you to make changes to the manuscript, if you want to. Their advice supports you in making your manuscript the best it can be.

Friendly Reviewers, Beta Readers, and Editors

Three types of supportive readers are friendly reviewers, beta readers, and professional editors. "Friendly reviewers" is a term coined by Stephen B. Heard in *The Scientist's Guide to Writing* that I'm borrowing here because it well describes those supportive readers who serve as proxies for your preliminary readers.[1] Friendly reviewers might be your friends who know your work well, or they might be trusted colleagues in the fields you want to reach. Like the anonymous peer reviewers solicited by your publisher, friendly reviewers read from a place of expertise. They should be qualified to comment on whether your engagement with the existing literature is sufficient, whether your research methods are suitable, and whether your arguments are compelling in the context of ongoing scholarly conversations in your field. You may also seek out certain friendly reviewers who are skilled at identifying structural or stylistic problems. Essentially, friendly reviewers can let you know how they would evaluate your text for publication if they were standing in the peer reviewers' shoes. And like peer reviewers, they may suggest changes to both the substance and the presentation of your manuscript. You can engage friendly reviewers before submitting your manuscript for peer review, or you can engage them later on to supplement the expert opinions of your peer reviewers.

Beta readers serve as proxies not for your expert preliminary readers but for your end readers. Beta readers don't necessarily have strong editorial skills or expertise on your subject matter. Rather, beta readers are valuable because they can tell you how they personally respond to the text, giving you a preview of how your end readers would receive your book if it were to be published in its current form. I engaged many beta readers for this book because, although I had helpful feedback from expert reviewers, I wanted to know whether people who weren't experts on scholarly writing and editing would be able to understand and implement my method for manuscript development. I shared my full manuscript with the beta readers before my last round of manuscript development (Moment 3, as described in Chapter 1) and asked them to tell me what resonated with them, what caused confusion or begged further explanation, and what elicited a negative response. I didn't expect them to assess the text or provide editorial suggestions, but merely to read it and let me know their immediate reactions to the various chapters.

The same individual might read your manuscript in different ways and offer different kinds of feedback depending on the expectations you establish when asking them to respond to your work. Without direction, many readers default to presenting feedback as a series of immediate reactions to the text; you've experienced this kind of feedback if you've had someone read your draft, mark it up as they went, and turn those notes over to you unfiltered. Such unfiltered feedback is useful from a beta reader, but less helpful if you're trying to get a high-level editorial view of how argument, evidence, structure, and style are working across the text. Although you can't be too demanding of someone who is volunteering their time to help you, you can be clear about the scope of feedback you're hoping to receive from a supportive reader before they sit down to read your manuscript. Make sure your supportive readers also understand that you're still developing your manuscript and therefore line editing and copyediting won't be helpful to you at this stage.

The third type of supportive reader is a professional editor. Professional editors bring a wealth of experience from working with many previous texts in your genre. Although they may not always be experts on your specific topic, they are experts on the construction and publication of scholarly books and likely have a good sense of what will make a book successful with readers. I count acquiring editors and series editors in this category, though the amount of support they're able to offer authors can vary (as discussed in Chapter 1). A freelance developmental editor can thus also be a valuable optional member of your manuscript development team. Because professional support of this nature is unfamiliar to many academic authors, I want to spend the rest of this appendix explaining what's involved in working with a freelance editor. You'll be better equipped both to decide whether working with a freelance developmental editor is right for you and to seek such help if you want it.[2]

Working with a Freelance Developmental Editor

A scholar may seek the help of a professional developmental editor for many valid reasons, and hiring a professional doesn't make you a bad writer or a lazy one. Your friends, colleagues, and mentors may not have the time, capacity, or skill to give you detailed developmental feedback, making qualified friendly reviewers and beta readers hard to come by. Nearly everyone in the neoliberal academy is making do with less time and fewer resources than are required to produce quality scholarship, including the time and resources to help others with their writing. Furthermore, if you're an introvert who struggles to ask people for favors, you may

shrink from enlisting others to do the work of reading and responding to your manuscript. Even if you have your go-to people
who are enthusiastic about helping you develop your ideas, they
may not be optimal readers for the same reason you may not be
an optimal reader of your own work. If they're already familiar
with your research, your stylistic quirks, and what you ultimately
want to say, they may not have enough distance from the text to
see where the blanks should be filled in.

Additionally, you may be wary of showing your work in progress to people who have a conflict of interest. Although feedback
from publishers and peer reviewers can be quite valuable in the
early stages of your manuscript development, you may only have
one shot to make a good impression with a publishing gatekeeper.
You may understandably hesitate to bring them a draft that you
already know needs significant improvement, even if you're not
yet sure how it should be improved. You may be similarly reluc-
tant to show underdeveloped work to people who have power
over your career, such as department chairs or colleagues who
will vote on your tenure case. Many scholars also fear that their
ideas will be stolen—or unintentionally borrowed—by other
writers who are then quicker to the publication pipeline. I don't
say any of this to discourage you from seeking feedback on your
work from trustworthy colleagues. But unfortunately, access to
such people can be inequitably distributed, with minoritized
scholars sometimes feeling they have fewer individuals they can
turn to for help. An impartial developmental editor who is not
currently an active scholar or gatekeeper in your field can be a
favorable alternative or supplemental source of support, although
it must be acknowledged that the financial resources needed to
secure such support aren't equitably distributed either.

Will your press or journal see it as "cheating" if they find out
you've worked with a developmental editor or plan to work
with one after peer review? Rest assured that people who work

in publishing are highly supportive of developmental editing because they understand and embrace the idea that producing quality books is a team effort. Publishers would likely offer professional developmental editing support to more of their authors if they had the means to do so. An acquiring editor may even have more confidence in your project's viability for publication if they're aware that you're willing to seek this kind of editorial support, because an author who seeks the aid of a developmental editor shows that they can set ego aside to make their text the best it can be for readers.

As for how your academic peers might perceive your use of developmental editing services, there may be some out there who think competent writers work in isolation to refine their manuscripts. But scholars have always depended on networks of support in various forms and, fortunately, more are becoming aware of the benefits and legitimacy of professional editing services. You also can help educate your peers; hand them this book if necessary. The one circumstance where it may not be acceptable to get the assistance of a professional editor is when you are a student preparing a paper or thesis for evaluation. If this is you, check with your instructor or supervisor to find out what kinds of assistance they consider appropriate and make sure any editor you enlist is aware of your situation.

When and How to Find an Editor

In Chapter 1, I discussed the key moments in the publication process at which manuscript development takes place. The assistance of a professional developmental editor can be sought at any of these moments: when preparing for initial submission to publishers; after receiving feedback from preliminary readers but before receiving publication approval; or when preparing the final manuscript to go into production. Different developmental editors may prefer to work with authors at different points in the process, so find out the preferences of any individual editors you're interested in working with. I recommend searching for a developmental editor as soon as you know you might want to work with one, even if you're a long time away from actually needing their services. Many experienced freelancers book up well in advance and may require several months' notice in order to accommodate your timeline.

Getting direct referrals from people you trust is the best route to finding a good developmental editor. The most valuable referrals come from those who have worked with the editor and experienced the benefits of their skill and working style first-hand. If you're already working with a publisher, your editor there may be able to recommend freelancers their authors have worked with successfully in the past. Social media sites and directories hosted by professional editing organizations such as the Editorial Freelancers Association or the Chartered Institute of Editing and Proofreading can also be good places to look for people who are publicizing their editorial services.

You'll then want to make sure any editor you're considering is qualified and a good fit for your project. Look at the editor's website and arrange a direct conversation if you need more information. Expect that any editor you contact will also want to gather information about you, your goals, and your timeline before agreeing to work with you.

What to Look for in a Professional Editor

The first thing you'll need to ascertain is what type of editorial support the editor offers and whether it matches the needs of your manuscript. There's no industry-standard definition of developmental editing, so you'll want to confirm that the editor is prepared to help you with argument, evidence, structure, and style, if those are the things you need assistance with. If you're looking for complementary services such as writing coaching or copyediting, find out if the editor offers those as well, though you should expect developmental editing to occur separately from other levels of editing.

Ask how the editor typically works with manuscripts and in what form you'll receive their feedback. As independent professionals, developmental editors are free to choose their own practices, and editors vary widely in how they do things. It's best to ask directly how they would work with you rather than to assume. I once spent weeks writing a detailed editorial letter for a client. I was proud of the letter's quality, but when I sent it to the client and her response was to ask where the track changes were on her document, I was horrified to realize that our expectations about the process and deliverables of developmental editing had been misaligned. After that, I always made sure that my authors understood the scope of my editorial work before I got started. If something isn't clear to you about an editor's process, ask.

Make sure that the professional support that your editor intends to provide will not shade into ghostwriting, that is, writing or rewriting part or all of your manuscript for you without being given credit as a coauthor. Although ghostwriting is common in trade publishing, especially when a book is authored by a celebrity or other figure who is not a professional writer, ghostwriting is not ethical practice in scholarly publishing. An editor may assist with presentational aspects of your text—such as titles, headings, transitional language, and more precise or standard wording that more clearly conveys your original ideas—but it's not acceptable for an editor to write their own ideas into your text. A freelance editor should demonstrate a strong awareness of ethical standards in scholarly publishing and know where to draw the line with your manuscript.

You'll also want to understand the experience and expertise that an editor brings to the table to make sure they're qualified to give you guidance applicable to your publishing context. Subject matter expertise isn't always essential, and it may be hard to find a professional editor who knows your topic and literatures as well as you and your academic colleagues do. More useful to you will be the editor's awareness of writing and publishing conventions in your field. They may have gained such awareness in a number of ways: by having a successful academic writing career themselves; by working in the academic publishing industry; or by working with many previous authors who published with the kinds of presses you're hoping to publish with.

Advanced degrees and formal professional credentials may or may not matter to you when selecting your editor. Some developmental editors have extensive academic training and may hold a terminal degree in a scholarly field. Some editors have completed professional training programs in editing and publishing. Neither academic training nor professional editing programs typically include specific courses on developmental editing of academic manuscripts, so practical editorial experience may end up being more important than a formal credential when it comes to the editor's skill at handling your manuscript.

Perhaps the most crucial thing to consider when evaluating whether an editor might be a good fit for you is whether their personality and approach to feedback meshes with your own. Some editors will be businesslike and direct when critiquing your manuscript, whereas others may be more attuned to authors' anxieties around having their work edited and take a gentler approach. Neither way is more correct; it's simply a matter of what you prefer. It's all right to acknowledge that you're sensitive to feedback or criticism and to choose a more empathetic-seeming editor for that reason. Be up front about your needs and what you hope to gain from the editing experience. This isn't to say that you should demand that an editor accommodate your every preference, but rather that it's better to establish before getting started that you and the editor are a good match. Many freelance editors will be happy to refer you to someone else if they realize they won't be a good fit for you.

Before agreeing to work with you, an editor may have a list of policies they want you to be familiar with, and they may even want you to sign a formal contract setting forth the conditions of the work they will do and their compensation. None of this should be taken as a red flag; rather it speaks to the editor's professionalism and experience because it shows they understand the procedures that are most likely to lead to a productive working relationship between them and their clients. Pay particular attention to any contract clauses that specify how the editor–client relationship can be terminated and what will happen to any funds exchanged if things fall through or you aren't satisfied with the editor's work. Feel free to ask for clarification, because the editor may have a sensible reason for a policy that you wouldn't have thought of.

Whatever the editor's process and personality are, you should always feel respected when interacting with them. They should recognize your expertise as a scholar, even if you need help presenting your ideas. If you feel intimidated, talked down to, or even disliked by an editor, they're simply not the right editor for you to work with. At the same time, recognize that professional editors are so accustomed to the process of developing manuscripts that they sometimes forget what it's like to be an author seeking help for the first time. It's reasonable for you to ask questions and admit what you don't yet know about the process of working with an editor. If you get the impression that an editor finds your questions annoying, they're probably not the editor for you. If you have doubts about working with a particular editor after speaking with them, thank them for their time and seek another editor whose style is a better fit.

Timeline and Costs

Having established process and personality fit, you'll need to verify that your editor can accommodate your logistic needs, such as your timeline for editing and your budget. Find out when the editor would be able to work with your manuscript and how long their work typically takes. Share your publishing timeline so the editor can figure out how and when their work might fit into your writing and revision schedule.

Consider the matter of cost too. As laborers with highly specialized skills, scholarly developmental editors don't give away their services cheaply. To give in-depth attention to an academic manuscript—to deeply understand how the text is constructed, accurately diagnose its needs, and offer an executable editorial plan—requires many hours of work, as you'll understand from reading this book. Most professional developmental editors are self-employed, so they charge rates that keep their businesses sustainable as a main source of income. You may not be aware of what budget will be required to work with a given editor, so it's reasonable to ask in advance what they would charge for a project like yours. If your editor charges by the hour, you'll also want to find out how many hours they usually spend on a manuscript like yours. They should be able to give you an estimated range, even if they can't answer definitively before digging into your manuscript. Expect that developmental editing of a full book manuscript could reach several thousand dollars, depending on the extent of work provided by the editor. If you prefer to work with a particular editor but their rates are out of your budget, avoid haggling or asking for discounts. Instead, ask whether the editor might be able to change the scope of their work to align with the funds you have available. You'll also want to find out when the editor requires payment and what forms of payment they accept.

Getting professional support undoubtedly requires a significant financial investment. Many scholars justify the expenditure because of the great value it offers: the support of a talented developmental editor will not only improve your manuscript, but it can also improve your overall quality of life by bringing new energy and insight to a major project. By improving your chances of accomplishing your publication goals, editorial support can also help you achieve career milestones—such as hiring or promotion in academic positions—which may in turn have monetary payoffs that more than offset the expense of hiring the editor. All that said, professional editing services are probably not worth going into debt for most people. Instead, explore alternative sources of funding.

If you have institutional funding such as research or start-up funds, you can likely have your university pay your freelance editor as an independent contractor. You may also be able to include editorial support as a line item in an external research grant, or apply for grant funds from your publisher if such funds are available. If you're writing a book with competitive market appeal, you may be able to negotiate an advance on royalties from your publisher before signing your book contract. This advance could then be applied toward outside editorial support. If you know that you'll want to seek the help of a developmental editor, I encourage you to discuss all possible options with your publisher before signing a contract. In some rare cases the publisher may be able to offer developmental editing, whether by an in-house editor or a freelancer, at no cost to you.

Ensuring Successful Relationships with Supportive Readers

No matter which kinds of supportive readers you decide to enlist in your manuscript development—whether friendly reviewers, beta readers, or professional editors—the most impactful thing you can do to ensure a successful working relationship is to communicate clearly with each other. Clear communication means letting your supportive readers know precisely what help you need from them and staying in touch when things change, such as if you want to push your timeline back. Misalignment of expectations is the foremost cause of disappointment and frustration between authors and those who try to support them.

One way to show gratitude for any support you receive is to stay in communication. Try to acknowledge receipt of feedback as soon as possible, but don't feel compelled to respond directly to the comments right away. Criticism and advice about your writing can be difficult to accept, even if you trust your reader and know they mean well. Take sufficient time to process the feedback for yourself and consider how it will help you move forward. If your reader has offered to have a follow-up conversation with you, schedule it promptly so as not to drag out the process too long. Inform your reader if you know it will take you a while to get to their comments. If you aren't sure whether your reader is open to discussing their feedback or to looking at your manuscript again after you've revised it, ask them directly while allowing for the possibility that they may not be available for additional rounds of feedback.

You have autonomy to decide which of your reader's suggestions you'll adopt and which you may prefer to modify or even reject. A good reviewer or editor will respect that you must write the text you want to write and that you may not follow all recommendations. However, a reader may find themselves frustrated or confused if you ask for additional feedback on a later version without incorporating the reader's previous suggestions. In such instances, you may want to explain your choices and show that you have taken their feedback seriously, even if you decided to diverge from it in some instances.

Your supportive readers will appreciate updates on the status of your publication. They will want to celebrate your accomplishments with you, so keep them in the loop when you receive positive peer reviews, have your manuscript accepted for publication, or submit the final version into production. Including the names of your supportive readers in your book's acknowledgments or sending them a physical copy of the published book is a wonderful way to honor the part they played in the development of your manuscript. I treasure such gestures from my developmental editing clients, and I know your supportive readers will too.

Using This Book's Method
to Support Other Writers

THE DEVELOPMENTAL skills taught in this book can be used not only by scholarly authors themselves but also by any editor, mentor, or colleague who provides feedback on another writer's text. This appendix addresses several potential readerships:

- Professors who mentor graduate students, advanced undergraduate writers, and early-career faculty
- Scholars who organize special journal issues or edited volumes
- Book series editors and journal editors
- Acquiring editors at scholarly publishers
- Peer reviewers
- Freelance editors and literary agents who work with scholarly authors

The guidance in this appendix draws heavily on my decade of experience working with academic writers as a professional developmental editor. I've intentionally kept the advice as broad as possible so that it will be useful to those in all the aforementioned roles.[1] You may need to adapt some of the tips according to your role, because a peer reviewer will respond to a manuscript differently than a dissertation advisor who will respond differently than a series editor, and so on. You can apply the bits that work for your circumstances and leave the rest for now. Experiment to figure out what leads to the best results for you and your authors. And if you lack the time to implement every step I recommend, the core principles should still be applicable to any manuscript development situation.

Setting Expectations

The primary thing you can do to ensure that your feedback is productive is to communicate clearly with your author about what manuscript development is, how it can help them on their path to publication, and why it must precede other forms of editing during the revision process. Give the writer an overview of the steps involved in manuscript development before you commit to working together. They should understand that you'll be gathering contextual information from them about their manuscript and publication goals. Assure them that you'll be reading their text thoroughly and assessing it for argument, evidence, structure, and style—the four pillars that are key to their manuscript's chances of moving forward to publication. The author should expect to receive a holistic editorial summary that lays out the major areas that can be improved and offers solutions for them to consider. If you intend to return their manuscript with itemized edits that support an overall editorial plan, inform the author of this as well.

Your author must understand each step of the process and what they will receive at the end so they aren't unnerved or disappointed by an approach to feedback that they weren't expecting. Explaining your method in advance also shows your authors that you care enough about giving useful feedback to have a systematic method. Your author will see that you're on their side and that you're investing substantial labor to help them achieve their publication goals. Make it clear that the purpose of the method is to arrive at a stronger manuscript, not to criticize the author or undermine their confidence.

Set expectations around the more practical aspects of your feedback process. You can anticipate and answer these questions up front:

- Would you like to receive the draft as a Word file, printed document, or some other format?
- Will you be providing an editorial plan in writing or would you prefer to meet with the author in person to discuss the plan after you've read their manuscript? Can a recording of that meeting be made and shared with the author?
- Should the author be prepared for multiple rounds of feedback and revision with you if necessary, or do you only have capacity to comment on their draft this one time?
- What condition do you expect their draft to be in when they send it to you? Are you happy to read something that looks more like an outline with notes, or do you want the draft to be further along?
- When in the author's publication timeline do you find it most helpful to offer feedback? Would you prefer to see the draft before initial submission to publishers or after peer review?
- How long should the author be prepared to wait between sending you their draft and getting your feedback?

Although some authors may have their own preferences about practical matters, I advise you to stick to the practices that work well for you. Instead of changing your feedback process in re-sponse to every author request, explain the rationale underlying your methods and be transparent about the labor conditions that shape the ways you're able to support authors. Your trans-parency is vital both for helping authors understand where you're coming from and for modeling sustainable editorial labor, which many of the writers you work with will need to engage in themselves someday.

One request I frequently receive as a developmental editor is for the author to send me their manuscript for feedback one chapter at a time rather than letting me read the entire manu-script at once. In the author's eyes, this arrangement allows them to work efficiently, making progress on some chapter drafts while I'm reading and responding to others. However, this workflow generally goes against the spirit of developmental editing, which addresses matters that reach across the entire text. If the book's core argument or chapter structure needs sig-nificant development, piecemeal feedback on individual chap-ter drafts won't be a good use of anyone's time. If an author wants to receive developmental feedback before the entire manuscript is complete, I might suggest to them that we work on their book proposal or an overview and outline of the book before looking at individual chapters. Regardless of the kinds of requests you receive from authors with respect to process, the key thing is to consider what is underlying the request and how you can honor the author's needs while also maintaining the integrity of the developmental editing process.

Once you and your author have aligned your expectations, proceed through the phases of manuscript development as de-scribed in this book. I'll now review the steps briefly, offering additional guidance specific to situations where you're working with a text that isn't your own.

Applying the Manuscript Development Method

Clarifying the Author's Mission

Before reading the author's manuscript, find out who the author is trying to reach with their text, how and where they want it to be published, and how the publication supports their broader professional ambitions. Make yourself aware of the conditions and constraints under which the author is working to develop their manuscript. All these factors can—and should—affect the feedback you give. Ask your author to fill out the Phase I questionnaire or use the questions to guide an in-person conversation. If you have concerns about the author's mission—maybe you realize that you won't be able to offer the support this author needs, or you have qualms about the author's vision—this is the time to bow out and point the author to someone else who can help them.

Assessing the Text

When assessing the manuscript, read it using the procedure outlined in Chapter 3. Any notes you take during the assessment step are just for you as you are forming your impression of the text's strengths and challenges. You won't share them with your author until you've had a chance to consider the text as a whole and repackage your notes into a constructive editorial summary.

One benefit of the systematic procedure for reading and marking up a text described in Chapter 3 is that it forces you to read attentively. Yes, giving someone else's manuscript this level of attention can be time-consuming and laborious. But reading attentively—especially before suggesting revisions—is a way of honoring the author's labor. If you don't have the capacity to carefully engage with an author's manuscript, consider whether you're really helping the author by agreeing to give them feedback on it. I've talked to many recent PhDs who were convinced that their doctoral committee didn't even read their whole dissertation before approving it. It's also disappointingly common for peer review reports to come back brief and include comments that make authors suspect the reviewer did not read the manuscript carefully before writing their report. I bring up these examples not to place blame on peer reviewers or graduate advisors, who are themselves often overworked and exploited by academic institutions, but rather to remind you that you have an opportunity to give an author's work careful attention that they may not receive anywhere else.

Crafting Your Editorial Summary

After assessing the manuscript, use your notes to synthesize an editorial summary as described in Chapter 8. Professional developmental editors write formal, detailed editorial letters for their authors that can run from ten to twenty pages or more for a full book manuscript. Depending on your role and your capacity, you may write a shorter letter or a more informal letter. I recommend writing a formal letter when you're giving manuscript feedback in the context of peer review or some other professional scenario where your editorial summary will be preserved for posterity and viewed by people other than you and the author. If you have a friendly, trusting relationship with your author, you might forgo a written summary altogether and present your editorial feedback in a casual conversation. If you go the less formal route, at least jot down key points to guide the discussion, because your feedback will likely be too extensive to hold in your head entirely.

When preparing your feedback for the author, use the template for editorial summaries provided in Chapter 8. In addition to the points outlined in the template, express both gratitude for the opportunity to read the author's manuscript and optimism about the text's potential, if possible. Mention an aspect of the text that you strongly connected with, or list some readerships or publishers that you think will be particularly drawn to the author's approach. Begin your feedback on a genuinely encouraging note so the author gets the sense that their efforts to develop the manuscript will be worthwhile.

It's also helpful to situate yourself for the author, reminding them of any aspects of your background or professional role that are coloring your feedback. If you and the author already know each other well, this might be less necessary, though it can still be helpful to flag for the author when your personal biases or expertise may be coming into play with specific pieces of feedback. For example, if you're reading the manuscript before peer review and you happen to have subject-matter expertise on the text's topic, you may be able to alert the author to items that you believe could raise concerns among reviewers in your field.

Accompany each development opportunity discussed in your editorial summary with a brief explanation of why pursuing that opportunity will help the author achieve their goals for the text. Remember, the purpose of giving feedback is not to criticize what the author has done but rather to support the author in getting to a more successful draft. You'll be diagnosing problems, yes, but your discussion of the problems should be geared toward giving the author language to understand how the manuscript could be made to work better. Referencing the author's goals in this way will both give them motivation to fix the problems and help them avoid making similar mistakes in the next round of revision and in any future manuscripts they write.

Pushing yourself to justify each development opportunity also keeps you honest about whether you may be unconsciously trying to impose your personal preferences about how manuscripts should be written. It's fine to share preferences with authors you're mentoring but recognize them as preferences— not rules. Try not to interfere with the author writing the manuscript as they want to write it. If you can't explain why a particular revision will help the author achieve their goals for the text, it may be that the revision isn't truly needed at all.

As you present development opportunities to your author, draw the author's attention to specific locations in the text where the opportunities can be found. If you've identified many opportunities of a given type and you're short on time, choose one or two examples to highlight in your summary and leave it to the author to find the rest. If you provide your author with an annotated copy of their manuscript that shows the itemized edits you recommend, reference a few of these edits—with page numbers—in your summary, so your author knows what to look for.

In addition to identifying the development opportunities in your editorial summary, also suggest concrete editorial solutions. Explain why the solutions you're offering will both address the identified problem and help the author achieve their goals for the text. For example, if one chapter is way too long, instead of saying "Chapter 4 is 7,000 words too long, you'll need to make cuts," say something like this:

> Your chapter lengths are largely consistent, except for Chapter 4, which at 22,000 words is about 7,000 words longer than the others. Readers and publishers in your field often expect

chapters to be about equal in length and no longer than 15,000 words. You could reduce the length of Chapter 4 by moving the material on France to Chapter 2 and removing the Italy case study entirely. The point of Chapter 4 will come across well enough with only the West Germany case. Cutting the Italy material will also help your total word count stay down, as I know you're trying to stay within the 100,000-word limit stated in your publishing agreement.

Providing justification for your editorial advice helps build the author's trust in your perspective, making them more receptive to your suggestions. Explanations equip the author to come up with an alternative solution that addresses the underlying issue, even if they don't want to take your particular suggestion during revision. The author in the preceding example might decide they would prefer to keep the Italy and France material in Chapter 4 but cut the West Germany case study. Either route would solve the core length issue.

You may fear that the number or severity of problems you identify in a manuscript will cause your editorial summary to feel overly negative or discouraging to the author. In such cases, you might lead with each solution or suggested edit before pointing out the problem it's intended to solve. Position these solutions as general developmental strategies that all manuscripts can benefit from, and then talk about the specific ways in which your author's text will be improved by implementing these revisions. This framing may help your author avoid interpreting criticisms as a personal attack on their shortcomings as a writer. Instead, you'll be teaching them new techniques to improve their work.

The author must decide when and how to implement the edits you suggest, but you may want to complete your summary by advising the author on next steps. Many authors appreciate a checklist they can use to guide their revisions. If your author is short on time or capacity, it will be helpful for them to know which development opportunities you believe are most pressing and which might be saved for a later stage or skipped altogether without severe consequence. If the text needs more development than the author might have been expecting or might indeed be able to execute in the time they have available, remind the author of their stated goals for publication. You may be able to persuade them that the time and labor is worth investing, even if it means asking for an extension from their publisher or redirecting attention away from other projects. Inversely, you may help them realign their goals to be more realistic under the present conditions. In any case, authors appreciate seeing that you've kept their goals in mind when formulating your editorial summary. End your summary on a positive note, reaffirming your author's agency to make choices about their manuscript and your faith in their ability to improve the text.

Annotating the Text

If you have time, supplement your editorial summary with specific comments, queries, and suggestions embedded in the manuscript draft that will help your author execute the plan outlined in your editorial summary. Start with a fresh copy of the manuscript and follow the procedure for itemizing edits laid out in Chapter 9. Do not simply return to them the draft that you marked up with your own notes when you did your assessment read-through. Those notes captured your initial reactions to the text as you read it, but unless your author has specifically asked to see your initial reactions, it will be more helpful if you filter and synthesize those reactions, bringing them into alignment with your editorial summary. The annotated text you give back to your author should be an intentional documenting of places where an edit is recommended or a selection of examples that demonstrate to the author the kinds of edits you're recommending across the manuscript. Also note spots where the text is especially effective and needs no further development.

Be as precise as possible when suggesting edits. Although one-word comments jotted hastily in the margins may be adequate when recording initial impressions for yourself, such comments will likely not support your author in actually improving their text. For example, you may think that a particular passage should be condensed because it repeats material that has already appeared in the text. Rather than highlighting the passage and commenting "Condense," try a comment like this:

> The first four sentences of this paragraph feel repetitive with the paragraph that begins this section. You could cut these sentences and move the final sentence of this paragraph up to become the final sentence of the first paragraph in the section.

In other words, spell out what needs fixing and how to fix it so your author can proceed with their edits efficiently and with confidence that they are improving the text for good reason. If you've already spelled out the nature of the issue in your editorial summary, reference your summary directly in your embedded notes. For instance, if your summary described a general opportunity to reduce length by eliminating repetition, you can use the shorthand "cut due to repetition, as noted on page 4 of editorial summary" when noting specific edits.

Precision is particularly helpful when suggesting the addition of new material. Indicate the exact location where new text should be inserted, or as exact as you can get, and specify the approximate length of the text that will satisfy the underlying need. Is a whole new section or chapter needed, or could the problem be addressed with just a sentence or two? When scholarly authors hear feedback such as "add an explanation of X," they may assume that several pages of material are needed along with extensive citations of the scholarly literature. If that seems necessary, go ahead and say so. But if what you're suggesting can be accomplished in a few words or a single paragraph, letting your author know this can save them time and make them feel less overwhelmed by the work ahead.

Sometimes you won't be able to make a precise editorial suggestion without more information from the author. In such situations, use productive queries to guide the author toward an appropriate revision solution of their own devising, but don't use questions to avoid providing meaningful feedback. If you're tempted to ask, "Is this explanation needed?" it will be more helpful to unpack the editorial thought process behind your question. Consider a comment along the lines of "I suspect that most members of your intended readership will already understand this concept and won't need three full paragraphs of explanation. Are there other reasons why you've decided to include this material?" This kind of query will allow your author to make an informed decision about what to do with the passage in question.

If you find yourself writing comments like "I don't understand the point of this passage," or "I find the tone off-putting here," consider whether centering your own personal experience of the text is helpful for your author. It could be, if you happen to be a member of the author's intended readership. In most cases, however, it will be more helpful to articulate why the author's intended readers may struggle to understand the point of a passage or why they might be put off by the author's tone. Stylistic edits are particularly important to review before communicating them to your author, since stylistic preferences are often both personally subjective and culturally conditioned. Centering the author's goals and intended audiences can lead your author to more effective editorial solutions rather than dwelling on your own negative reaction to the text.

It's perfectly understandable if you don't have the time or capacity to provide in-text comments to the standard outlined here. If you won't be able to give your initial notes a once-over to ensure that you're only sharing useful, explanatory comments with your author, plan to present the author with an editorial summary only. The best way to honor your author's time and effort is to let them know that you're unable to give more detailed feedback rather than burdening them with the task of decoding and filtering your knee-jerk reactions to the text.

When editing at the developmental level, it will rarely be appropriate for you to make direct changes to the author's manuscript, unless you're a professional editor who's been explicitly enlisted to reshape the text. The work of revision is the author's responsibility, and they may reasonably want to modify or reject some of your editorial suggestions. You may think it would be more efficient and helpful to make some edits yourself, but your author may find such intervention presumptuous if they haven't asked for it. It is more respectful of the author's agency to explain a suggested edit and allow them to execute the edit as they see fit. This also saves them the time of figuring out whether you've made direct changes yourself and undoing them if necessary. If you think your author may be happy to have you provide hands-on editing of their manuscript, confirm this up front when setting expectations about the editorial process.

Finally, resist the temptation to line edit or copyedit the author's manuscript at this stage. The author is still developing the major pillars of their manuscript, and the text is still in flux. Making lower-level suggestions or corrections across the manuscript that have little bearing on matters of argument, evidence, structure, and style will be a poor use of your time while potentially demoralizing your author and distracting them from the most significant tasks at hand. If you identify recurring grammatical or mechanical issues that you think should be brought to the author's attention, make note of them in your editorial summary or annotate a couple examples in the text itself, but remind your author that such matters are best dealt with after developmental editing is complete.

Returning Feedback and Following Up

Before returning your editorial summary and annotated manuscript draft to your author, review everything to ensure that you've

- kept your author's mission in mind;
- presented your suggested edits in a way that allows your author to accept, reject, or modify them;
- explained your reasoning for each suggestion when possible;
- offered positive reinforcement when applicable;
- stayed within the scope of developmental feedback, that is, avoided copyediting and excessive line editing which could distract or overwhelm your author; and
- adequately addressed any specific areas of concern that the author has discussed with you while not unduly dwelling on anything the author has asked you not to focus on.

Verify that your recommended edits are clearly stated and straightforward to execute. Double-check that none of your suggestions contradict each other or would be impossible to implement simultaneously. If you've ever had a peer reviewer or editor tell you to significantly shorten a manuscript while also suggesting the addition of extensive new material, you know how frustrating such instructions can be. Provide some editorial direction as to how all the development opportunities you've identified can be addressed harmoniously, or acknowledge that trade-offs may be necessary, and leave it to the author to decide which opportunities they will pursue.

I recommend taking one final pass through your comments to modulate them for tone. Your author may be feeling vulnerable and anxious in anticipation of receiving your feedback. They may interpret your criticisms as more severe than you intended them to be, especially when put in writing. Your goal is to help your author improve their manuscript and bring it closer to publication, so an empathetic, positive tone that expresses faith in their ability to successfully revise—even if revision is difficult—will likely be more effective than a tone that betrays frustration with or disappointment in what the author has produced so far.

Striving for an encouraging tone doesn't mean that you can only say nice things about the author's work. You owe the author an honest assessment, and you won't be serving them well if you refrain from sharing information that could help their project be more successful with publishers and eventually readers. Find a balance to avoid overwhelming your author or crushing their enthusiasm for their manuscript. You want your author to understand that you are on their side and cheering for their success, even if a lot of work remains to be done.

If you have a vested interest in the publication of the author's manuscript (for instance, you're a series editor or acquiring editor who wants the author to develop their manuscript further so you can publish it), be direct about which aspects of your editorial feedback are open-ended suggestions and which are more like requirements if the author wants to publish their manuscript with you. Although I recommend being as direct as possible to prevent misunderstandings about what the author needs to do to move forward, your feedback can still show your support for the project. For example, if you're an in-house editor who knows from experience that certain developmental issues tend to jeopardize manuscripts with peer reviewers or your press's editorial board, explain this to your author so they understand that your aim is to set them up for success with readers at the next stage of the process.

When returning written feedback to your author, let them know how and when you'd like to follow up with them. You may want to meet for a conversation shortly after sharing your editorial plan; many authors find such conversations helpful as a way of processing written feedback and envisioning a path forward. Some authors are so anxious about having their work evaluated, even by a trusted supporter, that they won't look at the feedback, let alone act on it, until prompted. You can help your author expedite the revision process by scheduling a conversation to discuss the editorial plan as soon as possible.

Providing Multiple Rounds of Feedback

If you're willing to provide additional feedback after the author revises the manuscript, once again set clear expectations with your author. Setting expectations around additional feedback might mean suggesting a deadline for the author to get a revised draft to you and letting them know what your next round of feedback will focus on. If you're not able or willing to provide additional feedback, be clear about that too. If your role entails enforcing submission deadlines, let the author know when you'll need to receive a revised version and what could happen if they miss the deadline.

When you receive the revised manuscript from the author, you may be disappointed to find that it hasn't improved significantly. You can troubleshoot this situation in a few ways. First, try communicating your next round of feedback in a different style or format to help the author absorb it. Some people do better with talking out potential solutions rather than reading them in a letter. Second, if you've been couching your suggestions gently, be more direct. Some people benefit from having a clear plan of action rather than being presented with open-ended questions or many alternative paths to choose from. Third, consider whether you are asking too much from the author in each round of development. It may help to concentrate on one issue at a time in your feedback and to prioritize the most serious developmental problems before discussing others.

If you've tried these techniques and your feedback is still not leading to improvement, it may be that you and the author are not a good match or that they need more support than you're able to give. If you're an in-house editor who feels that the manuscript still has strong potential to be published despite its problems, you may want to refer your author to a freelance editor or coach who can give them more attention than you're able to (point the author to Appendix C in this book). Clearly communicate your expectations and requirements to consider the manuscript at a later date so the author can take these to the freelancer and use them to guide revisions.

Set clear boundaries around how much feedback you're able to give, especially when an author wants to keep coming back to you with revised drafts. No one can be an infinite source of editorial aid. You can also support your author by encouraging them to break away from endless cycles of perfectionistic revision. For some authors, it feels safer to keep working on the manuscript with someone they trust than to send it off to a publishing gatekeeper who might criticize or reject the work. At some point, the kindest thing you can do for your author is let them know the time has come to submit and get feedback from the people whose evaluations count the most, even if the prospect is intimidating.

I'll end this appendix with an underdiscussed aspect of providing feedback to authors on their writing: One of the traits that makes a good editor—empathy—can also carry emotional costs. It is easy to get so invested in an author's success that you spend more time with their manuscript than you intended or internalize your author's anxieties and stresses. You may also become frustrated or even angry if your author opts not to take your editorial advice. You may be disappointed if your author doesn't achieve their publication goals, despite those outcomes often being far beyond your control. Find your own strategies for maintaining the necessary emotional distance from your authors and their manuscripts so that your practice of support remains sustainable in the long term.

Ultimately, each author and manuscript is unique, so you'll have a unique editorial experience each time. If you keep these general principles in mind and build on them as you gain your own experience and hone your own editorial style, you'll be equipped to handle whatever comes up.

NOTES

Introduction

1. For more detailed discussions of the various levels of editing, including developmental editing, line editing, and copyediting, see *Chicago Manual of Style*, 84–85; Ginna, *What Editors Do*; Greenberg, *A Poetics of Editing*, especially the chart on page 11; and the various contributions assembled in Gross, *Editors on Editing*.

2. Guides that can help you decode expectations for genres of academic writing other than books in the humanities and social sciences include Belcher, *Writing Your Journal Article in Twelve Weeks*; Booth et al., *The Craft of Research*; Heard, *The Scientist's Guide to Writing*; and Lai, *The Grant Writing Guide*.

3. For an extended discussion of the risks, both real and imagined, of sharing work in progress, see Richards, "Risk."

4. I recommend other guides that explicitly cover the conceptualization and drafting stages of scholarly writing, which this book does not. Discussion of book conceptualization can be found in Ginna, *What Editors Do*, 8; and Rabiner, "The Other Side of the Desk," 77–80. Knox and Van Deventer's *Dissertation-to-Book Workbook* offers a systematic method for the conceptualization of academic books, applicable beyond dissertations. Drafting a book proposal before writing your manuscript can also be a productive exercise in conceptualization and can save you from getting too far down the writing path with a concept that won't support a publishable book. If you're willing to try the proposal-first approach, Portwood-Stacer, *The Book Proposal Book*, can help. For specific tips on producing a new manuscript draft from scratch, see Belcher, *Writing Your Journal Article*, 390–400; Knox and Van Deventer, *Dissertation-to-Book Workbook*, 211–213; and Heard, *Scientist's Guide to Writing*, 59–75. Heard focuses on scientific papers, but his list of techniques for generating material for a first draft—such as word stacks, concept maps, and outlines—will be useful for all kinds of writers and manuscripts.

5. Two books to explore if you'd like to find more fulfillment in your writing practice are Evans, *Black Feminist Writing*, and Sword, *Writing with Pleasure*.

6. A select portfolio of books I've worked on as a developmental editor can be found at https://manuscriptworks.com/client-projects.

Chapter One: Three Moments for Manuscript Development

1. For more detailed discussion of the acquisitions process at scholarly book publishers and the various roles involved in making publication decisions, see Portwood-Stacer, *Book Proposal Book*, Chapter 1.

2. Cassuto, *Academic Writing as if Readers Matter*, 32.

3. In the interest of simplicity and retaining focus on the moments when manuscript development is appropriate, my discussion of the publishing process does not cover all possible scenarios an author might encounter. For more comprehensive discussion of the publishing process for scholarly books, see Portwood-Stacer, *Book Proposal Book*. See also Britton, "Thinking Like a Scholarly Editor"; Germano, *Getting It Published*; Herr, *Writing and Publishing Your Book*; Luey, *Handbook for Academic Authors*; and Miller, "The Book's Journey."

4. For further discussion of scholarly book series and communicating with both acquiring and series editors, see Portwood-Stacer, *Book Proposal Book*, 8–9, 30–34, and 105–121.

5. For more guidance on identifying publishers that are the most promising fits for your project, see Portwood-Stacer, *Book Proposal Book*, Chapter 1. In some cases, publishers are looking less for fit with previous offerings and more for fit with new areas of interest for the press. It can be hard to know about a press's nascent areas of growth from the outside, but you can give yourself a leg up by taking advantage of any opportunities to hear from editors and learn about their areas of acquisition.

6. This phenomenon is documented in Fyfe et al., "Untangling Academic Publishing." The report notes that the crisis in library funding dates to at least the 1980s and "did not blow over, but became the new normality" (p. 3).

7. For further guidance on the peer review process, see Association of University Presses, *Best Practices for Peer Review of Scholarly Books*.

8. For further discussion of advance contracts in the scholarly publishing context, see Portwood-Stacer, "Advance Contracts, Explained."

9. For more detailed guidance on writing a response to peer reviews, see Portwood-Stacer, *Book Proposal Book*, 122–134.

10. For further discussion of in-house manuscript development—or lack thereof—for scholarly books, see Ferber, "Of Monographs and Magnum Opuses: Editing Works of Scholarship," 198–199; and Shipton, "The Mysterious Relationship," 52–55. Editors not being able to give their manuscripts as much attention as they want to is not unique to academic publishing, nor is it new. Gerald Gross and several of the contributors to *Editors on Editing* (the last edition of which was published in 1993) note the already long-standing tradition of acquiring editors not having time in their workdays to provide developmental or line editing support to authors and having to perform such tasks on nights or weekends if they're able to do them at all.

Chapter Two: Delineate Your Goals, Timeline, and Capacity

1. For further guidance on researching publishers and assembling a list of comp titles, see Portwood-Stacer, *Book Proposal Book*, Chapters 1–3.

2. For a discussion of trade publishing in comparison with scholarly publishing, see Portwood-Stacer, "Trade Publishing for Scholarly Authors." For practical guidance on book publishing outside of scholarly publishers, see Friedman, *The Business of Being a Writer*, and McKean, *Write Through It*.

3. Cayley's *Thriving as a Graduate Writer* includes a chapter titled "Developing Sustainable Writing Habits" (pp. 160–168), in which Cayley outlines five common challenges that academic writers face and offers targeted strategies for each one. I appreciate Cayley's approach because she acknowledges that different strategies work for different temperaments and encourages experimentation. Belcher also offers an extensive list of "obstacles to writing daily (or at all)" in *Writing Your Journal Article* (pp. 31–32). A corresponding list of "Solutions to Common Academic Writing Obstacles" can be found on Belcher's website at https://wendybelcher.com/writing-advice/solutions-common-writing-obstacles/. Several other books provide further guidance on writing when time is limited: Boice, *Professors as Writers*; Hayot, *Elements of Academic Style*, 17–35; Jensen, *Write No Matter What*; Sword, *Air & Light & Time & Space*; and Zerubavel, *The Clockwork Muse*.

4. See Evans, *Black Feminist Writing*, especially pages 1–9, for a helpful accounting of "personal and professional stressors" experienced by many scholarly writers. I'm particularly grateful to Evans for naming the reality that national and global crises can affect writers' personal capacity to do their work.

5. Michelle R. Boyd's *Becoming the Writer You Already Are* is a good resource for writers experiencing "emotional and psychological blocks" (p. 12). I particularly appreciate Boyd's diagnostic schema that categorizes writing challenges as "Inherent, Institutional, and Interpretive" (p. 18) and further breaks down inherent challenges as being traceable to "the Head, the Hand, and the Heart" (p. 19). Stephen B. Heard's *Scientist's Guide to Writing* names "common behavioral challenges" and suggests techniques for "encouraging behavioral self-awareness" that may help you approach writing in a different way (pp. 22–29). He also offers tips on getting started with a new text (pp. 30–41) and keeping up your momentum (pp. 42–55). Heard's tools are beneficial even if you aren't writing in the sciences. Joli Jensen's *Write No Matter What* is another guide with honest and practical advice about confronting the "writing myths" that cause fear and other negative emotions that can prevent academics from enjoying and finishing their writing projects.

6. For tips on reconnecting with a writing project you've become disenchanted with, see Jensen, *Write No Matter What*, 77–81, 86–92. For guidance on deciding whether to abandon a writing project, see Jensen, *Write No Matter What*, 109–113,

and Portwood-Stacer, "Four Reasons to Keep Working on Your Book (and Four Reasons Why It's Ok to Quit)."

Chapter Four: Opportunities to Develop Your Argument

1. Miller, "The Book's Journey," 61.

2. For additional discussion of argumentation in scholarly texts, see Belcher *Writing Your Journal Article*, 66–82; Booth, et al., *The Craft of Research*, 101–167; Cassuto, *Academic Writing*, 50–54; Germano, *On Revision*, 81–109; Haag, *Revise*, 177–188; and Portwood-Stacer, *Book Proposal Book*, 54–61.

3. Belcher's discussion of claims for significance in contrast to arguments is worth reading in full in *Writing Your Journal Article*, 191–198.

Chapter Five: Opportunities to Develop Your Evidence

1. Herr, *Writing and Publishing Your Book*, 76–77.

2. For more specific advice on crafting opening hooks, and discussions of other types of hooks beyond anecdotes, see Sword's chapter, "Hooks and Sinkers," in *Stylish Academic Writing*, 76–86.

3. For additional discussion of image selection and use, see Herr, *Writing and Publishing Your Book*, 86–95. The use of images can raise both developmental and practical concerns. If you want to use images that are protected under someone else's copyright, you'll need to request permission from the rights holder to reprint them, and you may have to pay a fee. Any original images such as maps, diagrams, or tables may have to be professionally redrawn before they can be included. In many cases you—not your publisher—will be the one to shoulder the costs involved, so check your publishing agreement to see what image-associated costs you're responsible for as the author. If you haven't signed a publishing agreement yet, bring up incorporating images into your book beforehand, because your publisher may be able to cover the costs. Or you might decide to save money and administrative effort by eliminating any visuals that aren't integral to the reader's experience of your text.

4. For more guidance on ensuring alignment between evidence and claims, see Knox and Van Deventer, *Dissertation-to-Book Workbook*, 13–17. For further discussion of logical reasoning and how to acknowledge and respond to potential reader objections, see Booth, et al., *Craft of Research*, 154–167.

Chapter Six: Opportunities to Develop Your Structure

1. Norton, *Developmental Editing*, 111–112.

2. For guidance on writing an annotated table of contents, see Portwood-Stacer, *Book Proposal Book*, 68–76.

3. Several other books provide guidance on how to find a fitting organizational scheme for your manuscript at the chapter level. Booth et al., *Craft of Research* (p. 181), furnishes a few potential ordering principles—such as simple to complex, more familiar to less familiar, general to specific, and so on—that can be used on any type of scholarly manuscript. Herr, *Writing and Publishing Your Book* (pp. 9–10), offers typical templates for scholarly nonfiction book structures and walks through a method for figuring out a manuscript's argument and how the structure of the text can be brought in line to support it. See Knox and Van Deventer, *Dissertation-to-Book Workbook* (pp. 22–31, 95–109), for exercises on brainstorming potential organizing principles and selecting the most appropriate one for your book based on the material you have.

4. For further discussion of reverse outlines, see Cayley, *Thriving as a Graduate Writer*, 133–139. Knox and Van Deventer offer an alternative method for reverse outlining in *Dissertation-to-Book Workbook* (pp. 178–189).

5. Schrag, *Princeton Guide to Historical Research*, 279–281.

6. I've developed a structural template for scholarly book introductions after helping many authors who struggled to organize their thoughts for this kind of chapter in particular. See Portwood-Stacer, "How to Write an Introduction for an Academic Book."

7. For further discussion of typical book components, see the *Chicago Manual of Style*, 4–44, esp., 27–38. Hayot, *Elements of Academic Style*, offers additional tips and perspective on book introductions (pp. 89–101) and conclusions (pp. 130–139).

8. Booth et. al, *Craft of Research*, 176.

9. The principle that effective signposts shift the labor of navigating the text from the reader to the writer is articulated particularly well by editor Jenny Tan in her essay, "The Problem with 'I argue that . . .'"

10. For additional tips on crafting effective titles for your book and chapters, see Hayot, *Elements of Academic Style*, 140–148; Norton, *Developmental Editing*, 75–78; Portwood-Stacer, *Book Proposal Book*, 77–81; Schrag, *Historical Research*, 368–373; and Sword, *Stylish Academic Writing*, 63–75. For additional thoughts on headings, see Norton, *Developmental Editing*, 220–221. On topic sentences see Cayley, *Thriving as a Graduate Writer*, 51–53; and Schrag, *Historical Research*, 294–298.

11. If you're still struggling to wrap your head around effective versus ineffective signposting, I recommend Cayley, *Thriving as a Graduate Writer*, 45–49, and Cassuto, *Academic Writing*, 73–76.

12. More discussion of breaks (paragraph breaks, specifically) and transitional language can be found in Cayley, *Thriving as a Graduate Writer*, 49–55, and in Hayot, *Elements of Academic Style*, 102–115.

13. Additional advice on reducing manuscript length can be found in Haag, *Revise*, 189–205.

Chapter Seven: Opportunities to Develop Your Style

1. On the use of academic writing style to portray a particular academic persona, see Becker, *Writing for Social Scientists*, 24–38.

2. For numerous rhetorical templates that can be used to put your ideas in conversation with those of others, see Graff and Birkenstein, *They Say/I Say*.

3. For additional tips on balancing quoted material with your own voice and eliminating unnecessary citations, see Booth et al. *Craft of Research*, 201–207; Cassuto, *Academic Writing*, 40–49; Haag, *Revise*, 146–176; Hayot, *Elements of Academic Style*, 154–163; Herr, *Writing and Publishing Your Book*, 85–86; and Knox and Van Deventer, *Dissertation-to-Book Workbook*, 190–198.

4. Sword, *Stylish Academic Writing*, 173.

5. Atwood, *Underground*, 97.

6. Irani, *Chasing Innovation*, 19–20.

7. Portwood-Stacer, *Book Proposal Book*, 83.

8. Many if not most books on academic writing address the matter of jargon, so you'll easily find plenty of further advice on this topic. The most helpful resource, in my opinion, is Helen Sword's *Stylish Academic Writing*, which provides a list of questions to ask yourself about your reasons for including specific instances of jargon. Sword encourages writers to "retain only those jargon words that clearly serve your priorities and values" (p. 121).

9. Atwood, *Underground*, 3.

10. "Bullshit qualifications" is the term Becker uses in *Writing for Social Scientists* (p. 9) for instances of such softening, while Booth et al. call them "hedges" in *The Craft of Research* (p. 121). The decidedly more neutral terminology of Booth et al. speaks to their nuanced position that "pat certainty" can be just as damaging to a scholar's credibility as excessive timidity. They conclude their discussion of hedges by acknowledging that, "different research communities use hedges to different degrees, and finding the right balance is a matter of experience. So notice how experts in your field hedge their arguments and do likewise" (p. 122).

11. Booth, et al., *Craft of Research*, 120.

Chapter Eight: Draft Your Editorial Summary

1. Waxman, "Line Editing," 163.

Chapter Nine: Itemize Your Edits

1. If you find yourself overwhelmed by the prospect of moving multiple blocks of text around within your manuscript, you may find the system described by Scott Norton in *Developmental Editing* (pp. 147–148) helpful. Norton's system involves

making a table or spreadsheet to keep track of all text that is cut or moved during editing. In the table, each passage that is cut or relocated is associated with its page numbers in the original draft. This system ensures that no text gets lost in the cut-and-paste shuffle, and it also allows you to go back to your deleted text and repurpose it at a later time. Just remember to save a copy of your original draft before editing it so that the pagination reflected in the table is preserved.

Chapter Ten: Alter Your Text

1. Witte, "This Needs Just a Little Work," 99.

2. For further discussion of what's entailed in line editing, see *Chicago Manual of Style*, 84, and Witte, "This Needs Just a Little Work." For practical guidance on line editing your own academic prose, see Becker, *Writing for Social Scientists*, 71–81; Belcher, *Writing Your Journal Article*, 308–328; Booth, et al., *Craft of Research*, 252–71; Cayley, *Thriving as a Graduate Writer*, 56–126 and 140–157; Haag, *Revise*; Hayot, *Elements of Academic Style*; Heard, *Scientist's Guide to Writing*, 157–201; Pyne, *Voice and Vision*, 127–152; and Sword, *Stylish Academic Writing*. Bear in mind that much advice on style reflects what Rachael Cayley in *Thriving as a Graduate Writer* calls the "preferences and peeves" of the advice-giver and can be a form of gatekeeping that both "misunderstands the way language changes" and is consciously or unconsciously meant to "preserve a particular sort of cultural power" (pp. 79–80). Many line editing guides are available, so to avoid being overwhelmed, I recommend choosing one or two that resonate best with your own writing ethos. For what it's worth, Cayley's guide was the one I personally turned to when I needed to line edit this manuscript.

3. For further information about what's involved in copyediting, see *Chicago Manual of Style*, 84–109; and Saller, "Toward Accuracy, Clarity, and Consistency."

4. For an example of an academic publisher's manuscript preparation guidelines for authors, see those of Princeton University Press at https://press.princeton.edu/resources/prepare-and-submit-your-manuscript.

5. During production, your publisher will likely require your assistance with several additional noneditorial matters, such as image preparation, seeking applicable permissions to reproduce copyrighted material, and providing information to be used by the marketing and publicity staff at your press. For guidance on these matters, see Luey, *Handbook for Academic Authors*, 188–208, and Portwood-Stacer, *Book Proposal Book*, 135–147, in addition to any specific resources provided by your publisher.

6. For additional detail on professional copyediting as part of the editorial and production process at scholarly publishers, with particular attention paid to the "social dynamics" of the author–copyeditor relationship, see Einsohn, "Juggling Expectations." See also Shipton, "The Mysterious Relationship," 44–7. For a deeper dive

into the work of professional copyeditors in general, see Einsohn, *Copyeditor's Handbook*, and Saller, *Subversive Copy Editor*.

7. For instructions on indexing, see *Chicago Manual of Style*, 953–1005.

Conclusion

1. Becker, *Writing for Social Scientists*, 111.

Appendix C: Supportive Readers in Manuscript Development

1. Heard, *Scientist's Guide to Writing*, 216. Heard's chapter on friendly review offers many helpful tips on identifying potential reviewers and making good use of their feedback. Coincidentally, Heard served as a friendly reviewer for this book and offered me numerous insights from his perspective as an expert in scientific writing and publishing.

2. For additional advice on finding and working productively with professional editors, see de Keijzer, *How to Enjoy Being Edited*. For additional insights into how professional developmental editors work, see Norton, *Developmental Editing*, and Gross, "Working with a Free-Lance Editor or Book Doctor."

Appendix D: Using This Book's Method to Support Other Writers

1. For those seeking specific guidance on working with academic authors as a freelance developmental editor, including information on running a sustainable academic editing business, I offer a number of resources at my website, https://manuscriptworks.com.

BIBLIOGRAPHY

Association of University Presses. *Best Practices for Peer Review of Scholarly Books.* 2022. https://peerreview.up.hcommons.org/.

Atwood, Blake. *Underground: The Secret Life of Videocassettes in Iran.* MIT Press, 2021.

Becker, Howard S. *Writing for Social Scientists: How to Start and Finish Your Thesis, Book, or Article.* 3rd ed. University of Chicago Press, 2020.

Belcher, Wendy. "Solutions to Common Academic Writing Obstacles." Accessed November 16, 2024. https://wendybelcher.com/writing-advice/solutions -common-writing-obstacles/.

Belcher, Wendy. *Writing Your Journal Article in Twelve Weeks: A Guide to Academic Publishing Success.* 2nd ed. University of Chicago Press, 2019.

Boice, Robert. *Professors as Writers: A Self-Help Guide to Productive Writing.* New Forums Press, 1990.

Booth, Wayne C., Gregory G. Colomb, Joseph M. Williams, Joseph Bizup, and William T. Fitzgerald. *The Craft of Research.* 5th ed. University of Chicago Press, 2024.

Boyd, Michelle R. *Becoming the Writer You Already Are.* SAGE Publications, 2022.

Britton, Gregory M. "Thinking Like a Scholarly Editor: The How and Why of Academic Publishing." In *What Editors Do: The Art, Craft, and Business of Book Editing,* edited by Peter Ginna. University of Chicago Press, 2017.

Cassuto, Leonard. *Academic Writing as if Readers Matter.* Princeton University Press, 2024.

Cayley, Rachael. *Thriving as a Graduate Writer: Principles, Strategies, and Habits for Effective Academic Writing.* University of Michigan Press, 2023.

The Chicago Manual of Style. 18th ed. University of Chicago Press, 2024.

de Keijzer, Hannah. *How to Enjoy Being Edited: A Practical Guide for Nonfiction Authors.* Bell Buoy Press, 2023.

Einsohn, Amy. *The Copyeditor's Handbook: A Guide for Book Publishing and Corporate Communications.* 3rd ed. University of California Press, 2011.

Einsohn, Amy. "Juggling Expectations: The Copyeditor's Roles and Responsibilities." In *Editors, Scholars, and the Social Text*, edited by Darcy Cullen. University of Toronto Press, 2012.

Evans, Stephanie Y. *Black Feminist Writing: A Practical Guide to Publishing Academic Books*. SUNY Press, 2024.

Ferber, Susan. "Of Monographs and Magnum Opuses: Editing Works of Scholarship." In *What Editors Do: The Art, Craft, and Business of Book Editing*, edited by Peter Ginna. University of Chicago Press, 2017.

Friedman, Jane. *The Business of Being a Writer*. 2nd ed. University of Chicago Press, 2025.

Fyfe, Aileen, Kelly Coate, Stephen Curry, Stuart Lawson, Noah Moxham, and Camilla Mørk Røstvik. "Untangling Academic Publishing: A History of the Relationship between Commercial Interests, Academic Prestige and the Circulation of Research." May 25, 2017. https://doi.org/10.5281/zenodo.546100.

Germano, William. *Getting It Published: A Guide for Scholars and Anyone Else Serious about Serious Books*. 3rd ed. University of Chicago Press, 2016.

Germano, William. *On Revision: The Only Writing that Counts*. University of Chicago Press, 2021.

Ginna, Peter, ed. *What Editors Do: The Art, Craft, and Business of Book Editing*. University of Chicago Press, 2017.

Graff, Gerald, and Cathy Birkenstein. *They Say/I Say: The Moves that Matter in Academic Writing*. 6th ed. Norton, 2024.

Greenberg, Susan L. *A Poetics of Editing*. Palgrave MacMillan, 2018.

Gross, Gerald. *Editors on Editing: What Writers Need to Know about What Editors Do*. 3rd ed. Grove Press, 1993.

Gross, Gerald (Jerry). "Working with a Free-Lance Editor or Book Doctor." In *Editors on Editing*, 3rd ed., edited by Gerald Gross. Grove Press, 1993.

Haag, Pamela. *Revise: The Scholar-Writer's Essential Guide to Tweaking, Editing, and Perfecting Your Manuscript*. Yale University Press, 2021.

Hayot, Eric. *The Elements of Academic Style: Writing for the Humanities*. Columbia University Press, 2014.

Heard, Stephen B. *The Scientist's Guide to Writing: How to Write More Easily and Effectively throughout Your Scientific Career*. 2nd ed. Princeton University Press, 2022.

Herr, Melody. *Writing and Publishing Your Book: A Guide for Experts in Every Field*. Greenwood, 2017.

Irani, Lilly. *Chasing Innovation: The Making of Entrepreneurial Citizens in Modern India*. Princeton University Press, 2019.

Jensen, Joli. *Write No Matter What: Advice for Academics*. University of Chicago Press, 2017.

Knox, Katelyn E., and Allison Van Deventer. *The Dissertation-to-Book Workbook: Exercises for Developing and Revising Your Book Manuscript.* University of Chicago Press, 2023.

Lai, Betty. *The Grant Writing Guide: A Road Map for Scholars.* Princeton University Press, 2023.

Luey, Beth. *Handbook for Academic Authors: How to Navigate the Publishing Process.* 6th ed. Cambridge University Press, 2022.

McKean, Kate. *Write Through It: An Insider's Guide to Publishing and the Creative Life.* Simon Element, 2025.

Miller, Nancy S. "The Book's Journey." In *What Editors Do: The Art, Craft, and Business of Book Editing,* edited by Peter Ginna. University of Chicago Press, 2017.

Norton, Scott. *Developmental Editing: A Handbook for Freelancers, Authors, and Publishers.* 2nd ed. University of Chicago Press, 2023.

Portwood-Stacer, Laura. "Advance Contracts, Explained." May 11, 2022. http://manuscriptworks.com/blog/advance-contracts-explained.

Portwood-Stacer, Laura. *The Book Proposal Book: A Guide for Scholarly Authors.* Princeton University Press, 2021.

Portwood-Stacer, Laura. "4 Reasons to Keep Working on Your Book (and 4 Reasons It's OK to Quit)." April 26, 2020. https://manuscriptworks.com/blog/worth-it.

Portwood-Stacer, Laura. "How to Write an Introduction for an Academic Book" February 25, 2019. https://manuscriptworks.com/blog/intro-template.

Portwood-Stacer, Laura. "Trade Publishing for Scholarly Authors." March 6, 2024. https://manuscriptworks.com/blog/trade.

Pyne, Stephen J. *Voice and Vision: A Guide to Writing History and Other Serious Nonfiction.* Harvard University Press, 2009.

Rabiner, Susan. "The Other Side of the Desk: What I Learned about Editing When I Became a Literary Agent." In *What Editors Do: The Art, Craft, and Business of Book Editing,* edited by Peter Ginna. University of Chicago Press, 2017.

Richards, Pamela. "Risk." In *Writing for Social Scientists,* 3rd ed., by Howard S. Becker. University of Chicago Press, 2020.

Saller, Carol Fisher. *The Subversive Copy Editor: Advice from Chicago (or, How to Negotiate Good Relationships with Your Writers, Your Colleagues, and Yourself).* 2nd ed. University of Chicago Press, 2016.

Saller, Carol Fisher. "Toward Accuracy, Clarity and Consistency: What Copyeditors Do." In *What Editors Do: The Art, Craft, and Business of Book Editing,* edited by Peter Ginna. Chicago: University of Chicago Press, 2017.

Schrag, Zachary M. *The Princeton Guide to Historical Research.* Princeton University Press, 2021.

Shipton, Rosemary. "The Mysterious Relationship: Authors and Their Editors." In *Editors, Scholars, and the Social Text*, edited by Darcy Cullen. University of Toronto Press, 2012.

Sword, Helen. *Air & Light & Time & Space: How Successful Academics Write*. Harvard University Press, 2017.

Sword, Helen. *Stylish Academic Writing*. Harvard University Press, 2012.

Sword, Helen. *Writing with Pleasure*. Princeton University Press, 2023.

Tan, Jenny. "The Problem with 'I Argue that . . .'" *Feeding the Elephant: A Forum for Scholarly Communications* (blog). July 28, 2021. https://networks.h-net.org/node/1883/discussions/7982424/problem-i-argue.

Waxman, Maron L. "Line Editing: Drawing Out the Best Book Possible." In *Editors on Editing*, 3rd ed., edited by Gerald Gross. Grove Press, 1993.

Witte, George. "This Needs Just a Little Work: On Line Editing." In *What Editors Do: The Art, Craft, and Business of Book Editing*, edited by Peter Ginna. University of Chicago Press, 2017.

Zerubavel, Eviatar. *The Clockwork Muse: A Practical Guide to Writing Theses, Dissertations, and Books*. Harvard University Press, 1999.

INDEX

Page numbers in italic indicate illustrative material.

academic writing
    drafting stages, 227n4
    early career scholars, 68
    four pillars of, 3–5, *4*, 30, 57
    and ideological commitment,
      103
    methodological approach, 5
    stereotype of, 98
acquiring editors, 23–25, 139
    and developmental work, 29,
      229n10
American Society for Indexing, 150
analysis in text, 75–77
anecdotes as hooks, 75
appendixes, 86
arguments
    clarification of, 3, 58–60
    core claims in marking text, 50
    definition of, 57
    development of, 56–68
    editing phase, 123
    evidence, connections to,
      70–71, 127
    hidden, 59
    importance of, 57, 138
    main concepts, defining, 65–66
    main vs. subordinate, 60–62

    original perspectives, 56–57
    portability of, 63–65
    questions concerning,
      59–60
    and reader interests, 66–68
    in sample editorial summary,
      177–78
assessment phase, 7, 47–48
    marked-up text, sample,
      166–67
    reading like an editor, 49–55
    support for other writers,
      213–14
    timeline for, 51–53
assessment questions
    arguments, 59–60, 62, 65
    breaks and transitions, 93
    chapter structure, 82
    checklist of, 159–64
    evidence, 71, 74, 77
    length of text, 96
    main concepts, 66
    notes, 102
    organizational conventions,
      87, 91
    original ideas, foregrounding
      of, 101

assessment questions (*continued*)
    reader interests, 68
    section and paragraph level of
        organization, 85
    sentence-level clarity, 110
    tone, 106
Atwood, Blake, 104–5
author questionnaires and clarity of
    mission, 30–33, 43–45

Becker, Howard, 151
Becoming the Writer You Already Are
    (Boyd), 229n5
Belcher, Wendy, 60
beta readers, 197–98. *See also* readers
Black Feminist Writing (Evans), 229n4
booksellers, 24–25
Booth, Wayne C., 232n10
Boyd, Michelle R., 229n5
breaks and transitions, 91–93
breaks in text, closing up, 136–37
"bullshit qualifications," 232n10

capacity, writers', 41–42
Cassuto, Leonard, 20
Cayley, Rachael, 229n3, 233n2
chapter level
    reorganization in editing
        phase, 124
    in sample editorial summary,
        184–88
    structural chart, 168–72
    structure, 79–82, 231n3
Chartered Institute of Editing and
    Proofreading, 201
Chasing Innovation (Irani), 105–6
The Chicago Manual of Style, 144
"claims for significance," 60–62.
    See also arguments
conclusions, 86

concrete language, 104. *See also*
    vocabulary
contracts: clarity on details, 39–40, 139
copyediting, 144–45
    professional, 146–48
The Craft of Research (Booth et al.),
    232n10
cuts, 134, 136, 141

design, page-level, 147–48
developmental editing, 9
    itemization of edits, 131–40
    next steps following, 143–46
    support for other writers,
        213–24
    timeline and costs, 205–7
    See also freelance develop-
        mental editors; manuscript
        development cycle
Developmental Editing (Norton),
    232–33n1
developmental editors, 3, 119–20,
    198–207. *See also* editorial summaries
due dates, 39, 44. *See also* timelines

Editorial Freelancers Association, 201
editorial summaries, 119–30
    action plan, prioritized, 127–30
    essential sections, 121–25
    and itemized plan, coordina-
        tion, 136–40
    praise, 125–26
    reasons underlying problems,
        analysis of, 126
    sample, 174–89
    support for other writers,
        214–18
editors
    acquiring editors, 23–25, 139
    copyeditors, 146–48

developmental editors, 3,
    119–20, 198–207
managing editors, 146
production editors, 146
series editors, 23–25
as supportive readers, 198
See also freelance develop-
    mental editors; manuscript
    development cycle
Editors on Editing (Gross, ed.),
    228n10
edits
    avoidance of during
        assessment phase, 7, 52
    blocks of text, rearranging,
        135–36, 137
    changes, essential types of,
        132–37, 133
    coordination of summary and
        itemized plan, 137–40
    cuts, 134, 136, 141
    editorial plans, 116
    "hierarchy of changes," 128
    insertion of new material,
        133–34, 134
    itemization of, 131–40
    itemized, in sample editorial
        summary, 190–93
    planning and executing, 7,
        115–17, 141–50
    prioritization of, 127–30
    rewriting/reframing, 134, 135
    space in text, 136–37
    See also editorial summaries;
        manuscript development
        cycle
emotion and tone, 103, 111–13, 229n5
emotions, negative, 48. *See also*
    encouragement for writers
empathy, 226

encouragement for writers, 48, 111–13,
    151–53
    praise for, 125–26
    tone in comments on other
        writers' texts, 223
endnotes, 101–2
end readers, 19–21, 32–33
English as an additional language for
    writers, 145–46
Evans, Stephanie Y., 229n4
evidence, 3
    amount required, 72–74
    analysis of, 75–77
    connection to arguments,
        127
    development of, 69–77
    editing phase, 123–24
    impact of, 138
    in marking text, 50
    methodology, description of,
        73–74
    necessary for each argument,
        70–71
    from other writers, 73
    in sample editorial summary,
        178
expectations
    concerning argumentation,
        61–62
    concerning length, 94–95
    of readers, 20–21, 67, 69–70,
        74, 87
    setting of, 210–12, 224–25

feedback, 122, 139, 195–96
    multiple rounds of, 224–26
    on other writers' texts, 222–24
    in sample editorial summary,
        177
    See also peer review

five-column charts. *See* structural charts

footnotes, 101–2

formal vs. informal writing, 103–4

freelance developmental editors, 40, 198–207

   locating and evaluating, 200–205

   payment of, 206–7

   See also developmental editing

friendly reviewers, 196

frustration, coping with, 52–53. *See also* encouragement for writers

ghostwriting, avoidance of, 202–3

goals

   clarification of, 35–38

   in editorial summaries, 122

   reevaluation of, 128–29

   in sample editorial summary, 176–77

   See also mission

Gross, Gerald, 228n10

Haimson, Oliver, 63–64

headings and titles, 87–91

Heard, Stephen B., 196, 234n1

"hedgy" language, 108, 232n10. *See also* vocabulary

Herr, Melody, 71

"hierarchy of changes," 128

hooks, at beginning of book/chapters, 75

ideological commitments, 103

image selection/development, 76, 148, 230n3

indexing, 149

   working with professional indexers, 149–50

informal vs. formal writing, 103–4

insertion of new material, 133–34, *134*

introductions, 86

   in sample editorial summary, 183–84

Irani, Lilly, 105–6

jargon, 106–7, 232n8. *See also* vocabulary

Jensen, Helle Strandgaard, 165

"just-in-time" approach, 71

length

   sentence length, 108–9

   of text, in sample editorial summary, 181–82

   of text, modification of, 93–96

line editing, 143–46, 233n2

main arguments vs. subordinate arguments, 60–62, 65–66

main concepts, 65–66

managing editors, 146

manuscript development cycle

   author questionnaire, 30–33

   context and application, 9–12

   editorial summaries, 119–30

   itemization of edits, 131–40

   overview, 3–9

   peer review, 25–27

   phases of, 5–9, *6*, 19–22, *22*

   pre-submission development, 23–25

   publisher approval, 27–30

   support for other writers, 213–24

   supportive readers' roles, 195–208

   writers' roles, 9–12

   See also moments, key

manuscript preparation, 144–45
marginalized groups, writers from, 10–11, 41, 69, 152
markup
 annotating other writers' texts, 218–22
 authors annotating own texts, 49–55
 sample marked-up text, 166–67
 topical, 83
methodology, expression of in texts, 73–74
Miller, Nancy S., 56
mission
 author questionnaires and clarity, 30–33, 43–45
 authors' capacity and obligations, 41–42
 clarification of, 5–6, 17–18
 goals for book, 35–38
 of publishers, 23–24
 timeline, 38–40
 See also goals
moments, key, 8, 21, 23
 after approval for publication, 27–30
 after peer review, 25–27
 before submission, 23–25

narrative, impact of, 79–80
new material, insertion of, 133–34, 134
Norton, Scott, 79, 232–33n1
notes (endnotes or footnotes), 101–2

opportunities
 checklist for writers, 159–64
 contrasted with problems, 54–55
organizational conventions in texts, 85–91

departures from, 86–87
organization of text. See structure, development of
outlines
 in editorial summary, 124, 218
 reverse outline, 83
 See also structural charts

paragraphs
 line editing, 143–46
 paragraph level of organization, 82–85, 232–33n1
 structural charts, 173–74
passive voice, 107–8
peer review
 development after, 25–27
 peer reviewers, 25
 response to, 139
 See also feedback
perfectionism, 151–53
plagiarism, concerns about, 11
portability of arguments, 63–65
praise, 125–26. See also encouragement for writers
precision, importance of, 219–20
prefaces, 86
 in sample editorial summary, 183
preliminary readers, 19–21. See also readers
pre-submission development, 23–25
The Princeton Guide to Historical Research (Schrag), 84
problems vs. opportunities, 54–55
production editors, 146
production process, 146–50
pronouns, ambiguous, 109

publishers
    due dates, 39
    in-house processes, 228–29n10
    length requirements, 93–94
    marketing plans, 24–25
    mission of, 23–24
    potential publishers,
        evaluation of, 32, 37–38
    production process, 146–50
    working with, 13, 139

quotations
    balance between writer's
        voice/other research,
        99–100, 232n3
    used in text, 76

readers
    beta readers, 197–98
    creating connection with,
        105–6
    in editorial summaries, 122
    editors as supportive readers,
        198
    end readership, 19–21, 32–33
    external, 40
    friendly reviewers, 196
    goals concerning readership,
        36
    preliminary vs. end, 19–21
    reader experiences and
        organizational conventions,
        86–87
    reader interests and author's
        argument, 66–68
    readerships in sample editorial
        summary, 176–77
    supportive readers, 195–208
reorganization of text, 83

reverse outline, 83
reviewers, friendly, 196
rewriting/reframing, 134, 135

saving work, importance of, 141
scholarly writing. *See* academic
    writing
Schrag, Zachary, 84
The Scientist's Guide to Writing
    (Heard), 196, 234n1
scope of text, 31
secondary sources, 99–100
section level of organization, 82–85
sentence-level issues
    during development process,
        138
    line editing, 143–46, 233n2
    sentence length, 108–9
    style, 106–10
series editors, 23–25
    developmental work, 29
Sesame Street: A Transnational History
    (Jensen), 165
    editorial summary, 174–89
    itemized edits, 190–93
    marked-up text sample,
        166–67
    structural chart, chapter level,
        168–72
    structural chart, paragraph
        level, 173–74
signaling, of text's structure, 78
    in sample editorial summary,
        180–81
    signposting, 87–91
specialist terminology, 28, 106–7. *See*
    also vocabulary
structural charts
    chapter level, 80–81, 168–72

paragraph level, 83–84, 90,
   173–74
structure, development of, 3, 78–96
   breaks and transitions, 91–93
   impact of structure, 138
   organizational conventions,
      85–91
   reorganization, 83
   in sample editorial summary,
      179–82
   section and paragraph levels,
      82–85
   table of contents, 79–82
   text length, modification of,
      93–96
style, development of, 3, 97–110
   academic style, stereotype of,
      98
   in editing phase, 125
   impact of, 138
   informal vs. formal writing,
      103–4
   line editing, 143–44, 233n2
   notes, 101–2
   original ideas, foregrounding
      of, 99–101
   personal detail, 105–6
   in sample editorial summary,
      182–83
   sentence-level clarity, 106–10
   stylistic issues in marking text,
      50–51
   tone, 102–6
style guides, 144
   house style guides, 147
   Stylish Academic Writing
      (Sword), 232n8
sunk cost fallacy, 72–73
support

encouragement for writers,
   111–13, 125–26, 151–53
for other writers, 11, 209–26
problems vs. opportunities,
   54–55
supportive readers, 195–208
supportive readers, relationships with, 207–8
Sword, Helen, 104, 232n8

table of contents, 79–82, 231n3
terminology used in texts, 28, 106–7.
   See also vocabulary
text, marking up. See markup
text length, modification of, 93–96
thesis statements, 64. See also
   arguments
Thriving as a Graduate Writer
   (Cayley), 229n3, 233n2
timelines, 38–40
   for assessment phase, 51–53
   due dates, 39, 44
   institutional deadlines, 39–40
   key moments, 8, 21, 22
   See also moments, key
titles and headings, 87–91
tone, 102–6. See also style, development of
topical markup, 83
topics, 31. See also arguments
topic sentences, 88–91
transitions and breaks, 91–93
   transitional language, 92–93
Trans Technologies (Haimson), 63–64
typeset page proofs, 147–48

Underground: The Secret Life of
   Videocassettes in Iran (Atwood),
   104–5

vocabulary
    concrete language, 104
    "hedgy" language, 108,
        232n10
    specialist language/jargon,
        106–7, 232n8
    transitional language, 92–93
    vocabulary refinement, 28
voice, 99–100. *See also* style, development of

Waxman, Maron L., 128
Witte, George, 143–44
word choice. *See* vocabulary
word counts, 73, 94. *See also* length of
   text, modification of
writers
    capacity of individual writers,
      41–42

    challenges faced, 10–11, 41–42,
      111–13, 229n3, 229n4, 229n5
    English as an additional
      language, 145–46
    from marginalized groups,
      10–11, 41, 69, 152
    negative emotions, 48
    readers, creating connection
      with, 105–6
    support for other writers, 11,
      209–26
    voice, 99–100
    writers' roles, 9–12
    writers' roles in production
      process, 146–50
    writers' roles vs. editors' roles,
      120–21
    See also encouragement for
      writers

A NOTE ON THE TYPE

This book has been composed in Arno, an Old-style serif typeface in the classic Venetian tradition, designed by Robert Slimbach at Adobe.